BAPTISM AND CHRISTIAN UNITY

BAPTISM
AND
CHRISTIAN UNITY

by

A. GILMORE

LONDON
LUTTERWORTH PRESS

Printed in Great Britain by
The Camelot Press Ltd., London and Southampton

CONTENTS

1

INTRODUCTION

ARTICLE XXVII of the Church of England, dealing with baptism, concludes with the sentence, "The Baptism of young Children is in any wise to be retained in the Church, as most agreeable with the institution of Christ." That was in 1562. *Baptism and Confirmation*, a Report submitted by the Church of England Liturgical Commission to the Archbishops of Canterbury and York in 1958, however, stated that, "In the New Testament Adult Baptism is the norm, and it is only in the light of this fact that the doctrine and practice of baptism can be understood." The Report then proceeds to regard the baptism and confirmation of adults as the norm and to relate the pouring of the water to the making of the act of faith.

The Orthodox Creed of the General Baptists, published in 1678, not only speaks of baptism as the sign of the believer's fellowship with Christ in his death and resurrection, but goes on also to condemn "popish doctrine" associated with the practice of infant baptism. In Wales, however, in 1963, a Supplementary Report to *Towards Union* was published by the Joint Committee of the Four Denominations and dealt with baptism. It acknowledged the differences between the Baptists and the others, but went on to recommend that the United Church of Wales should provide for both forms of baptism and should receive as members those who have been baptized and who have made a personal and public confession of faith in Christ. All ministers of the proposed United Church should be free to administer either or both forms of baptism.

The bringing together of these quotations is just one indication of the changes that have taken place in the Church since the time of the Reformation. Some of the changes have come about as a result of bitter controversy; some as a result of practical considerations and some as a result of new insight into scripture and theology.

7

Within the last twenty-five years in Britain the change has been most marked, largely as a result of ecumenical encounter. But it is in other countries where traditions are less hardened that the changes have really come, and schemes of reunion planned for places like North India and Pakistan have shown much imagination in dealing with the problem of two forms of baptism within a united Church.

All this has meant a certain change of emphasis within the baptismal debate. On all sides it is agreed that the matter of infant baptism is not to be settled simply by reference to history. There is little doubt that the baptism of the New Testament was the baptism of believers, but this does not of itself prove the case. So that the ardent and well-travelled Baptist who reports that in Italy (or elsewhere) he has seen ancient baptisteries which so obviously provided for the immersion of adults may be speaking the truth, but it is not a truth which will carry much conviction in the present debate. Likewise the Anglican who argues a convincing case for the inclusion of infants in the households of Acts; maybe there were, but this too will not be regarded as relevant to the modern debate. What is thought to be relevant is not what the New Testament Christians did, but what they understood about baptism. Only when we have agreed on this can we proceed to consider the practice of baptism for the twentieth century. Biblical and historical theology must be the standards rather than simply the biblical records or the stories of history.

Changes of emphasis have also taken place on both sides of the debate. Within Paedo-Baptist circles the stress on original sin has been considerably modified, both in theory and in practice. There are still some mothers who fear lest an unbaptized child should die and be deprived of the glories of heaven, but their number must be diminishing rapidly, whilst there are few theologians who would want to argue seriously that the future of such a child was in jeopardy.

On the Baptist side there has been a modified emphasis

INTRODUCTION

on the mode of baptism in order to give an increased significance to the subjects of baptism. There is no giving on the point that a candidate for baptism must be a believer; but there is a tendency to agree that perhaps immersion is not the only way, even if it is still held to be the most symbolic way, and there are those who would maintain that it were better for a man to be baptized by affusion (or even sprinkling) than not to be baptized at all.

Perhaps one of the reasons why there are difficulties regarding baptismal theology is that the chief antagonists have not first done battle concerning the nature of the Church. In its extreme form the distinction is between those who believe the Church consists only of those who have been converted or have made a profession of faith and those who believe that such an expression of faith commits not only oneself but also one's children, at least to an act of initiation and training in the faith, later to be confirmed by a personal act of will on the part of the child himself. If you accept the first of these two alternatives then believers' baptism is inevitable, infant baptism is impossible, and any suggestion that a child who has not made his own response to the faith can belong to the Church is heresy. If, on the other hand, you accept the second of these two possibilities, then infant baptism is a help, believers' baptism is not ruled out (for there will always be those who were not baptized in infancy but who later come to faith and ask for baptism), and any suggestion that the family ought to be divided at this point will appear intolerable. If, to go on one stage further, it is thought that there ought to be some tie-up between Church and State, so that to be a member of the State is *ipso facto* to be a member of the Church, then infant baptism is inevitable.

Whilst it is probably not right that the Church should settle for either of these alternatives, there are nevertheless signs that both sides are trimming their sails somewhat, and it may well be that, if the ecumenical movement can be allowed slowly to pursue its course, some of these ecclesiastical matters will solve themselves, especially if the discussion on the nature of the Church could be more

9

ecumenical than the discussion that has taken place on the nature of baptism.

Already, however, certain changes in our understanding of the nature of the Church have produced some changes in our baptismal theology. When the Anglicans thought of themselves as a state Church, when to be a citizen of the earthly kingdom was to be a citizen of the heavenly kingdom, infant baptism was inevitable. Similarly, the concept of the gathered Church, by which to be a member of the Church was to be fully and wholly committed to a way of life, required an element of personal responsibility and ethics in the baptismal life. But today the Anglicans are less sure about the state Church and the Baptists are less sure about the gathered Church. At present no major changes in baptismal theology have come as a result, but it scarcely needs a prophet to see them round the corner. Within Anglicanism, for instance, it is admitted that there is considerable disquiet concerning the baptism of children whose parents themselves show little sign of Christian conviction. Will the day come when infant baptism will be reserved only for the infants of communicant members of the Church? Among Baptists, similarly, there are those who see the Church as wider than the wholly committed and as incorporating in some sense their immediate family. Will the day come when believers' baptism will be given this wider reference?

What we are trying to do in this book is to look first at two matters where there is frequent misunderstanding between Christians, and to examine some of the burning points of controversy, viewing them from the angle of the ecumenical movement and practice, rather than from the angle of theology, though clearly it is impossible fully to do one without the other.

The first matter is what we mean by faith. All Christians use the term and all relate it to baptism, but not all mean the same thing by it. Some see faith only as objective fact, others only as subjective experience. In recent years, British Baptists have tended to acknowledge the objective side of faith and baptism in a way that would have been foreign to earlier Baptist apologists who (to the non-Baptist at least) seemed to find the heart of the gospel in the subjective experience of converted believers, and in their experience of God rather than in the objective act of God who accepts sinners in Christ. But we need to pause first and ask what is meant by faith in this context, how it has been understood historically, and what our fellow Christians understand by it today. Until we have done this the misrepresentation of others, which is a feature of all parties to the debate, will continue.

When we have done this we shall then be the better equipped to deal with the other point of conflict, that of the relationship between faith and sacraments, or between the spiritual and the material. Recent theology has also forced this point on us by its emphasis on the incarnation and "the word made flesh", so issuing a challenge both to those who liked "the word" but not "the flesh", and also to those who were aware of "the flesh" but who had lost touch with "the word". So it is that most Baptists have had a fear (often emotional rather than rational!) of holy water and transubstantiation. So it is too that Anglicans and others have always been suspicious of any action which seemed to be interpreted only as a symbol and as an appendage to something which had already happened. The Baptist therefore has shuddered to hear the Anglican refer to his baptism, in which he became a member of the Body of Christ. And the Anglican has shuddered to hear the Baptist speak of being converted and becoming a Christian and then asking for baptism and church membership.

But again if we look at the thing historically it is doubtful whether these distinctions are as sharply defined as they appear when we meet to discuss them, as it were, from opposite sides of the fence. It is true, of course, that there are Anglican churches where infant baptism is practised with very little discrimination or pastoral care, and there are churches and public schools where confirmation has become something of a formality. But it is also true that this is not how Anglicanism at its heart has seen the sacrament, and increasingly today there is a body of opinion that is concerned about it. Similarly it is true that there are Baptists who see no connection at all between faith, baptism, the Lord's Supper and membership, and who practise each without any consistent regard to the others. But it is true also that in closed-membership Churches admission to membership is by baptism and is clearly stated to be so. And even in many open-membership Churches (where at times members are admitted without having been baptized by any Church at all) where members are baptized it is naturally assumed that their entry to membership is by means of baptism. They are not, as it were, admitted to membership on profession of faith and then baptized.

Moreover, there has been pressure for many years now among Baptists to relate the material to the spiritual through the sacramental. A. C. Underwood[1] was thought by many to have been over-stating his case when he wrote in 1947 that many English Baptists had then abandoned the merely symbolic view of the older generation in regard to baptism in favour of a more sacramental interpretation, but this would certainly be much more true today. And even earlier, it was the Baptist, H. Wheeler Robinson,[2] who drew attention to the connection between prophetic symbolism and Hebrew sacrifice, and who had for many years tried to relate prophetic symbolism to the sacraments. The fruits of the labours of these men have not yet ceased to appear among us.

In this respect the baptismal and theological debate has been considerably helped by medicine and psychology which has also seen a much greater inter-play between spiritual and material forces in the last generation. We need to glance at these as we pass by to see what they have to teach us lest

[1] *A History of the English Baptists*, 268 f. Cf. also his contribution to R. Dunkerley (ed.), *The Ministry and the Sacraments*, and R. C. Walton, *The Gathered Community*, 155 ff., for similar viewpoints, e.g. "Thus the Lord's Supper and Baptism are sacraments in which God acts and not merely ordinances which the Christian obeys." (p. 158.)

[2] "Hebrew Sacrifice and Prophetic Symbolism", in *J.T.S.*, (1942), 129 ff. Cf. *Old Testament Essays* (1927).

the Church should be the last place adequately and satisfactorily to relate the two worlds.

But not all the debate is at the theological level. Indeed
for many people it is not at the theological level at all. It
is at the level of practical churchmanship. Whilst each sect
remained within its ivory tower, and whilst each little
churchman remained in the same town and the same church
the practical issues did not loom so large. Today the world
has shrunk; people continually move from place to place;
education has taught us to question and investigate; and
missionary activities have led us to pastures where people
have never looked at things through our western denominational spectacles. Practical problems therefore have arisen
for Christians, and it is at these that we must look.

First there is the matter of the connection between
baptism and church membership. Among Paedo-Baptists
this may be an argument about baptism versus confirmation
or admission to full communicant membership. Among
Baptists it is just an argument about the relationship
between baptism and membership. There are those who see
the two as one, and there are others who see the two as two.
Historically, it is possible to find some support in Baptist
circles for both positions, and in between the two extremes
there is a wide variety of theory and practice, though increasingly the pressures of the ecumenical movement and
current theology are such as to strengthen the hand of
those who see baptism as the gateway to membership.
Negotiations between the Churches would certainly be
easier if all of one denomination accepted the same theology,
but this is day-dreaming. Probably the most we can do is
to see how this situation has arisen in the past by plotting
one or two milestones, and then hope that the rest of the
route will become clear as we seek to steer in company with
our brethren from other branches of the Church.

The second issue is that of re-baptism, and it is in some
ways the most thorny of all. Few subjects threaten the
ecumenical movement as far as Baptists are concerned
more than this one, and unless a start can be made with

charity rather than theology it would appear that no start
will be made at all. Here too, as in other places, it is of
course true that the forces are somewhat divided, and that
the suggestion that the re-baptism as believers of those who
have received baptism in infancy constitutes a blow at the
heart of the Christian faith has been hailed in some quarters
as the dawn of a new age; by others it has been mourned
as the end of an old era.

Theologically, the attitude that rejects re-baptism is im-
peccable. One can only look forward to the day when what
is theologically sound will be wholly practicable. But until
that day dawns it might be a good thing for all of us to
admit anomalies and pastoral exceptions. If both sides could
show a willingness to do this, then progress might be possible,
and already signs of hope are appearing. A generation ago
it would have been almost impossible for Baptists to discuss
re-baptism, since this in itself would have been tantamount
to admitting that what had taken place previously (by
sprinkling in infancy) was indeed baptism when they were
quite sure it was not. Moreover, the hammering out of
schemes of church union have shown that all is not lost, and
at the British Faith and Order Conference, 1964, it was
beginning to be acknowledged that in any truly united
Church both forms of baptism would have to co-exist.
Therefore what once seemed an insuperable barrier to union
is in fact being considered. The question is no longer
"Whether?" It is "How and when?"

Thirdly, and perhaps here the Baptist case is weakest of all,
there is the matter of the place of children in the covenant.
There is plenty of evidence that some Paedo-Baptists are
concerned about indiscriminate baptism and about the
status of children baptized but not subsequently kept within
the fellowship of the Church by parents who are not themselves practising members of the Church and by god-
parents who are either incapable of fulfilling their promises
or indifferent to them. One might have thought that this
kind of problem was one which Baptists successfully evaded
by the deferment of baptism until a later age, but this in

turn only presents more forcefully the matter of the relationship of the child to the Church. When one also acknowledges, as Baptists do, the place of infant dedication within the Church, the problem is further raised, for now one has to determine whose children are to be dedicated, and what is to be the difference between those who are dedicated and those who are not. The history of infant dedication among Baptists is by no means clear, although recent investigations suggest that the practice has in fact a longer history than we used to think. Several attempts have been made to give the practice a theology, and these are worthy of some examination by all who are concerned for Christian unity.

The most recent attempt suggests making a distinction first between believers (and their children) and unbelievers (and their children), followed by a further distinction between believers and their infant children. The former are those to whom the Word of God can be addressed, has been addressed, and from whom a response has been solicited; their children are then specially related to the Body of Christ by virtue of their birth.[1] As yet, few people have shown a willingness to come to grips with such a proposition and the general impression one gains, in private discussion if not in print, is that most people prefer to keep the rite they have been reared on, even if it has no theology behind it, and its meaning may be, to say the least, "shaky"— rather than undergo the ordeal of thinking the whole subject through afresh and perhaps finishing with something quite different, which would then have to be put over to one congregation after another. Such a reaction is perfectly understandable. But it is not the way victories are won.

Neither is it any more comforting to notice that certain other branches of the Church like to adopt the same attitude. It is, we realize, extremely difficult for Anglicans and others to consider modifications to anything so sacred as baptism, and therefore their problem is greater than the Baptist one. At the same time it is sad that they, too, so often refuse to

[1] This is the suggestion made by Neville Clark in *Christian Baptism* (pp. 321–3) edited by A. Gilmore, and will be discussed more fully later.

face up to the issue. It simply will not do just to say that the child of believing parents brought up in a Christian home should be regarded as the norm, unless one can go on carefully to explain how all this relates to baptism. Reactions to the recent Anglican report[1] also bear witness to a similar unwillingness to come to grips with this problem.

In short, Baptists want to stick to the rite they have, without being pressed to relate it to the child within the covenant; Paedo-Baptists want to continue to stand on the objectivity of redemption and the place of the child within the covenant, without being forced in any way to modify their doctrine of baptism.

In considering the matters outlined we shall try in each case to give some attention to the theology that has brought us where we are and to note the signs of change that have recently appeared. We shall then proceed to discuss them as practical issues, in the hope that by so doing we shall help the man in the pew, be he Baptist or Anglican, to see that there is a growing hope of a united Church with provisions for both forms of baptism.

[1] *Baptism and Confirmation*, S.P.C.K.

2

FAITH AND BAPTISM

Now that the ecumenical movement is bringing together the laity to discuss matters of Faith and Order, many of the traditional arguments and problems are coming out with regard to the connection between faith and baptism. On the one side there are those who seem to regard faith simply as a spiritual experience and baptism as an occasional appendage; on the other hand there are those who seem to believe that faith depends on baptism. Among the more sophisticated, one may even hear the phrases *sola fide* and *ex opere operato*. What do we mean by these phrases, and when we use them, how far do we take into account the thinking of the last twenty-five years of church history among the professional theologians? What in fact do we mean by faith in this context? And how has faith been understood by the reformers and leading thinkers in all the main streams of Christian life? These are the questions we shall try to understand and answer in this chapter.

A sympathetic approach to Paedo-Baptism is often regarded as suspect, or even objectionable, because it is alleged that it is a selling of the past in countenancing baptism without faith, when to Baptists baptism and faith have always been inseparable. In the discussions it is invariably said, or implied, that Baptists are the only people to hold to this principle and that all the other denominations go astray at this point. On occasions, those who try to be sympathetic are asked unequivocally to deny any belief in baptismal regeneration and to affirm that baptism without faith is meaningless, as if the simple addition of faith to baptism put everything right and brought the Baptist denomination back to where, in the opinion of its critics at any rate, it ought to be.

It is true, of course, that this has tended to be the traditional

Baptist position. Henry Cook,[1] for instance, says that baptism and the Lord's Supper, like the gospel, make an appeal to the soul on behalf of God, and according to the response of believing faith there comes the flooding in of the tide of grace. Then he goes on to assert that Baptists here are in a stronger position than any other Christian community because they insist, as the New Testament does, that the action of God on the soul of man in the sacraments, as anywhere else, is conditioned by man's response to the appeal that God is making for entrance. In the sacraments, for Baptists, the grace of God is mediated to believers only. Later[2] he goes on to assert that infant baptism preserves neither the historic gospel nor that emphasis on the need for believing faith which alone makes the gospel operative in the soul of man.

There Henry Cook is echoing the thought of the majority of Baptists, who would agree with him further when he goes on to suggest that all other forms of baptism tend to savour to some extent of magic. This is the position that Cullmann[3] has in mind when he says that the opponents of infant baptism often try to represent the matter as though every conception of baptism which does not postulate faith as pre-condition presupposes necessarily either a *magic* or a merely *symbolic* efficacy, and that the alternative of magic or symbol can be avoided only in the case of the baptism of adults, since in their case only a real and not a magical baptismal event is possible.

But of course Baptists are by no means the only section of the modern Church concerned to maintain a close relationship between faith and baptism, and to argue like this is to

[1] *What Baptists Stand For* (1947 edition), 72.

[2] *Op. cit.*, 174. That Henry Cook should have said this in 1947 is of course much less surprising than that he should have seen no reason to modify it when he presented his revised edition in 1961. In his appendix, *Infant Baptism in Recent Debate*, he tries to come to grips with Cullmann and the Church of Scotland, but because he is so concerned only with the personal faith of the person being baptized he does rather less than justice to the emphases on faith to which subsequently we shall draw attention.

[3] *Baptism in the New Testament*, 37.

do a disservice to the cause of truth. Let us look at the issues more carefully.

Luther, for example, had a high regard for the sacraments because he saw them to be a safeguard against two main errors: on the one hand, they were a safeguard against legalistic attempts to climb up to heaven (the error of the Papists), and, on the other hand, they were a safeguard against a purely spiritual religion with all the stress on the individual's "inward experience" (the error of the sectaries). What constituted the sacrament for Luther was the Word which accompanied it, though he made it perfectly clear that apart from faith the benefits of the sacrament were lost. What is offered can only be received in faith because it is not evident to the senses or capable of rational proof, and because it is not by any willing or doing of man that God is moved to speak his word of grace.[1] Thus, Luther's conclusion is that faith, though not necessarily part of the sacrament, is essential to the efficacy of the sacrament.

But then we have to ask what Luther meant by faith. He used the word *Glaube* in two senses. Sometimes he used it to mean historic faith, or the faith comprising the things that are believed. This was largely an intellectual matter and Luther demanded a kind of basic theological training for all Christians. Confirmation, which was more of an ecclesiastical "coming of age" and was neither sacramental nor episcopal, followed a two-year course of instruction concluding in a confession of faith.

At other times, however, Luther used the word to mean saving faith, or the faith by which we believe. This is the Christian's application to himself of the facts he has learned in the realization that Christ died for *him*. By faith, in this sense, the believer becomes one with Christ.[2]

When we proceed to ask next why and how this second kind of faith is to be related to infants it is unfortunate that Luther's writings become less clear. His insistence on infant baptism, in spite of his emphasis on personal faith, is due to

[1] P. S. Watson, *Let God Be God!*, 160–6.
[2] H. H. Kramm, *The Theology of Martin Luther*, 49–52.

Luther's desire to see salvation as being wholly of God, which is more easily seen when the candidate for baptism is a child and therefore a passive receiver than where he is an adult professing his faith.[1]

On how this works out, however, Luther is far less convincing and his teaching does not appear to be wholly convincing throughout his life. At times he seemed to suggest that the faith involved in baptism was vicarious faith and depended on the atmosphere of faith and prayer in which the child was presented. At other times, however, and increasingly so as the years passed by, Luther seemed to come more and more to the view that the child had a faith.[2] Beginning with his emphasis on the Word in the sacrament, Luther maintained that if the Word strikes on the ear it must subsequently be inwardly communicated to the spirit, and when Luther became confirmed in this view he then went on forcefully to assert that baptism without the personal faith of the person baptized is worthless.[3] Luther therefore accepted the baptism of infants because, rightly or wrongly, he had come to believe that infants can have faith, and whatever modern Lutheranism may make of the teaching of its founder, the fact nevertheless remains that it is not only the Baptists who have been fervent in this matter of relating baptism to a faith that is both personal and saving.

Those among the reformers who were unhappy about Luther's idea of attributing faith to a child were, however, equally concerned to maintain the link between faith and baptism. Bucer, for instance, had no desire to see a distinct separation of the sign of baptism and the grace concerned, as had Zwingli and the Anabaptists. He believed that the sacrament had a real, instrumental efficacy which depended on the faith of the recipient no less than on the divine election. Calvin, too, was concerned to stress that the

[1] For a collection of quotations from Luther to support this view, see J. Warns, *Baptism*, 140 ff.

[2] *Op. cit.*, 140 ff.

[3] *Greater Catechism*, 549. Cf. *Schwabach Articles*, 1529.

sacrament was ordained of God as a means of grace and that repentance and faith were indispensable to its proper use. By "faith" Calvin meant the knowledge of God as redeemer and the embracing of that knowledge by the mind, so that the final effect of faith was a firm trust in the salvation of God, though without making faith purely a human thing.[1] By "repentance" Calvin meant a real conversion of the life to God proceeding from a sincere fear of God.[2] Again, he saw this as more than simply a human turning aside from evil; rather was repentance to be regarded as following faith and belonging to it. Both were the work of the Holy Spirit and inseparable, save for the purposes of discussion. For Calvin, everything to do with man's salvation has its origin in the divine favour and initiative and not in any ability or activity of man.

All this suggests that the recipient of baptism is one who is consciously aware of what God has done for him and what he himself is doing for God. This, together with Calvin's firm attempt to move away from anything that savoured of magical notions of the sacrament, makes his retention of infant baptism something of a puzzle. His position is not very clear, and there are those who would attribute this to the fact that he and other reformers are trying to hold together two things which are mutually incompatible. They did nevertheless try, and there was obviously no intention on their part that the retention of infant baptism should in any sense lead to a separation of the twin ideas of faith and baptism.

After a careful survey of the writings of early Anglicans on the subject of baptism, G. W. Bromiley[3] concludes that the Anglican understanding of baptismal efficacy was essentially in the reformed tradition. The true work of baptism was not the outward washing of water, but (as both Cranmer and Ridley perceived) the corresponding inward washing of the Holy Spirit. The sacrament was a means of grace only as God used it as such to those who received it in

---

[1] Cf. *Institutes* III, ii. 35.   [2] See A. Dakin, *Calvinism*, 68.
[3] *Baptism and the Anglican Reformers*, 192–3.

faith. Moreover, baptism and faith did not ever need to be coincident in time, some people having faith before they received the sacrament whilst others had it afterwards.

Over the years, it is true, certain modifications have been made in baptismal doctrine in all these branches of the Church. Few Protestant theologians today, for example, still try to uphold Luther's arguments to prove that a child has faith, and consequently there has been an increasing tendency to lay the emphasis on the faith of the sponsors or on the faith of the local Church. In no case, however, has the element of faith been lost sight of; rather has it been re-interpreted.

Perhaps the best representative of this more modern reformed tradition is P. T. Forsyth,[1] who argues that although believers' baptism and infant baptism are psychologically different, they do have the main thing in common: the connection with the Word and its blessings in a faithful Church. In one case the experience precedes the act; in the other it follows (or it does not). In believers' baptism regard is had to the subject's past experience of the Word; in infant baptism it is to a further experience expected and provided for within the Church. "In adult baptism we are baptized *on* faith; in infant baptism *unto* faith; but both are justified by faith only."

In the case of Anglicanism, modifications of the reformed doctrines, as outlined by G. W. Bromiley, were certainly called for with the growth of the Oxford Movement in the early nineteenth century, and there is a tendency to imagine that at that point the Church of England went over to Rome, who (it is alleged) has never seen any link between faith and baptism except in a magical sense. Such an assumption is unfair both to Rome and to Canterbury, as we shall see presently.

Sufficient has now been said, we trust, to satisfy the reader that at the time of the Reformation and at any rate for a while afterwards there were many besides the Baptists who were concerned for faith as much as for baptism and for a close link between the two, though they were not agreed

[1] *The Church and the Sacraments*, 214.

precisely as to how the link should express itself. What about the attitude today?

In 1937 there was prepared for the Faith and Order Movement by a theological commission a book called *The Ministry and the Sacraments*, edited by Roderic Dunkerley, in which there were collected and compared the theological convictions of representatives of all the major Christian denominations. The items of agreement were later embodied in a Report with only the Orthodox members failing to give unqualified assent. One such item of agreement stated that the efficacy of the sacraments lies in the fact that "by means of them Christ, through the Holy Spirit, effects his Grace in the soul". It is then further stated that with this belief Christians exclude the erroneous idea that the sacraments are a refined form of magic; the recipient's attitude of faith is a necessary condition of the sacrament.[1]

Moreover, there has been an increasing tendency of late to acknowledge that within the New Testament faith is directly related to the act of baptism, and the faith in question is the faith of the person baptized.[2] A few examples will suffice. In 1923 W. M. Clow[3] wrote that according to the New Testament baptism was valid only when accompanied by faith. Within twenty years the Methodist scholar, H. G. Marsh,[4] wrote at length to the effect that within the New Testament the emphasis always rested on the faith of the candidate rather than on the rite, and his fellow Methodist, W. F. Flemington,[5] produced an abundance of evidence to show that the two ideas most frequently linked with baptism in *Acts* are those of "hearing the word" and "believing", and that in the Epistles baptism is linked with justification, sanctification and the new life.[6]

[1] This is summarized in J. R. Nelson, *The Realm of Redemption*, 121 f.
[2] For much of what follows see my article, "Some Recent Trends in the Theology of Baptism", in *Baptist Quarterly*, 15 (1953–54), 311 ff.
[3] *The Church and the Sacraments*, 26.
[4] *The Origin and Significance of New Testament Baptism*, 189 ff.
[5] *The New Testament Doctrine of Baptism*, 49, 110, 116. Cf. W. F. Flemington, "An Approach to the Theology of Baptism", in *Expository Times*, lxii (1950–51), 357.
[6] *Op. cit.*, 55 ff., 99 f.

It was at this point that Karl Barth[1] declared that New Testament baptism is always a response to faith and answers the desire for a sealing of that faith, and E. Brunner[2] attacked the contemporary practice of infant baptism as scandalous and maintained that baptism was not only an act of grace but just as much an act of confession stemming from the act of grace. Anglicans, such as the Bishop of Derby,[3] similarly, were beginning to acknowledge that from the beginning Christian initiation was linked with the forgiveness of sins and was followed by a new way of life, whilst the Archbishops' Commission on Baptism, Confirmation and Holy Communion[4] said that the note of personal response was conspicuous in the theology of initiation in the New Testament, and E. J. Bicknell[5] in his interpretation of the Thirty-Nine Articles says that, in scripture, baptism signifies the public acknowledgement of Jesus as Lord, and the blessings of baptism flow from the union with Christ thus gained.

Possibly the best of modern writers to treat of the matter theologically and to express it simply is Alan Richardson.[6] Writing of justification, he says that in order to avoid misunderstanding it would be as well if we did not speak of justification by faith, but of justification by faith and baptism, or of baptismal justification, "for there is no Christian baptism where there is no faith in Christ, and there is no justification apart from baptism into Christ's body". Dealing later[7] with the matter of baptism, he points out that it would have been quite impossible for the mind of the apostolic Church to have thought of baptism apart from faith, as an *ex opere operato* initiation ceremony. The New Testament has no answer to the question of the standing of a person who has been baptized, perhaps as a matter of social

[1] *The Teaching of the Church Regarding Baptism*, 42.
[2] *The Divine-Human Encounter.*
[3] A. E. J. Rawlinson, *Christian Initiation*, 7, 24.
[4] *The Theology of Christian Initiation*, 12.
[5] *A Theological Introduction to the Thirty-Nine Articles of the Church of England*, 466 ff.
[6] *An Introduction to the Theology of the New Testament*, 238.
[7] *Op. cit.*, 347.

or family custom, but who possesses no real personal faith, for in a missionary situation such cases do not arise; the apostolic Church would not have regarded anyone who had gone through the ceremony of being baptized without making a genuine response of faith as having been effectively baptized at all.

That last sentence makes it clear that when these writers speak of faith there is not much doubt that they are concerned with the faith of the person who is being baptized and not with the faith of his sponsors or the local Church. Moreover, the kind of faith that they have in mind is more than intellectual assent; it is a total response involving the knowledge of forgiveness, the acceptance of Jesus as Lord, followed by a new way of life.

All this seems to be weighty evidence[1] in favour of the way Baptists have viewed baptism from the beginning of their history; to have it from the pens of such eminent scholars of other denominations seems to confirm beyond a peradventure what they have always believed.[2] Whilst assuring the Baptists that in so far as they have only been concerned in reproducing the New Testament situation they have in fact interpreted the New Testament aright, it also takes some ground from under their feet by emphasizing that there are many other branches of the Church who also recognize this and are anxious to preserve it. Yet the baptismal controversy seems no nearer solution. Either these people, having found faith and baptism together in the New Testament, are now content to see them apart in the modern age, or else there is more to this conception of faith and baptism than the New Testament (because of its missionary situation) or the Baptists (because of the denominationalism) have been able to appreciate. The former of these two alternatives is not true. We must therefore take up the latter.

[1] It may be supported further by reference to Sanday & Headlam, *The Epistle to the Romans* (I.C.C.), 153 f., 162 f., C. H. Dodd, *The Epistle to the Romans*, 86 f., E. F. Scott, *The Pastoral Epistles*, 77, 176, V. Taylor, *Forgiveness and Reconciliation*, 136, and R. R. Williams, "Baptism", in A. Richardson (ed.), *A Theological Word Book of the Bible*, 27 ff.
[2] Cf. H. W. Robinson, *Baptist Principles*, 8, 13, 17, H. Cook, *What Baptists Stand For*, 105, 109 f.

Cullmann,[1] for instance, after asserting that Christian baptism without the operation of the Spirit is unthinkable, admits that this assertion could lead to the objection of magic, and proceeds to deal with this objection by introducing at this point the idea of faith, though he says it is the faith of the congregation assembled for baptism and not necessarily of the candidate for baptism. He then objects to the idea that this is vicarious faith, and denies that his idea is that the faith of the Church should do duty for a faith not yet present in the infant. The fact is that if faith were lacking in the congregation it would not be, strictly speaking, a congregation at all, and the Holy Spirit would be absent. Hence, without this element of faith, true baptism could not take place.

When Cullmann comes later to deal with the faith of the congregation more fully,[2] he declares again that this kind of faith (i.e. faith on the part of the congregation) is indispensable to the baptismal act and can be confirmed by the role played by faith in the New Testament in the miracles of Jesus, but he does not rule out the faith of the candidate as being unimportant. He thus reaches three conclusions about the relation between faith and baptism:

(a) *after* baptism, faith is demanded of *all* those baptized.
(b) *before* baptism, the declaration of faith is a sign of the divine will that baptism takes place, demanded from *adults* who individually come over from Judaism or heathenism, but in other cases lacking.
(c) *during* the baptismal act, faith is demanded of the praying *congregation*.

Many will feel that this approach to faith and baptism is quite inadequate, but there is nothing in it that Baptists would want to deny, and although it may go further than many Baptists would want positively to affirm, the attention paid to faith is such as to make it difficult for them to claim that they are the only ones who are concerned about this issue. There are other ways of interpreting the relationship

---

[1] *Baptism in the New Testament*, 41 ff.   [2] *Op. cit.*, 54 ff.

between faith and baptism besides the one to which they have become most accustomed.

In Scotland in recent years the element of faith has been preserved, if not actually revived. When the Scottish reports on baptism first appeared, the impression gained in some quarters was that their approach to baptism was even more Romish than Rome itself, but greater reflection shows an emphasis on faith which would be acceptable to many sections of the Free Churches if not to Baptists. Indeed the emphasis on faith, repentance and conversion is such that many people find difficulty in understanding how any of it can apply to infants.

We are told, for instance, that "baptism requires the response of faith, and a whole life of faith, for we cannot be saved without faith";[1] that baptism involves repentance,[2] and that apart from repentance and faith Christian baptism is unthinkable.[3] Those ideas are then related to the preaching of the Word, and it is stated that the gospel "calls men to account, to decision, and to confession of the Name of Christ, and all that is focused in Baptism".[4] The whole approach is Christocentric, and baptism into the name of Christ means baptism into the sphere where the mighty acts of God in the incarnation, the birth, life, death, resurrection and ascension are operative for our salvation.[5]

This Part I of the Report was subsequently revised in the light of comments and criticisms from Presbyteries and scholars throughout the world, and then re-issued.[6] This new document is somewhat shorter and clearer and, although not quite so detailed, is nevertheless built on the same foundations as the original. If anything, it tries to make more explicit just what we are meant to understand by faith. It is clear, for instance, that when the compilers of this Report stress the necessity of faith in baptism, they mean by "faith" much more than simply the response in

[1] *Interim Report of the Special Commission on Baptism*, Part I, 18.
[2] *Op. cit.*, 21.   [3] *Op. cit.*, 49.   [4] *Op. cit.*, 49–50.   [5] *Op. cit.*, 18.
[6] *The Biblical Doctrine of Baptism*. A Study Document issued by the Special Commission on Baptism of the Church of Scotland.

faith to the love of God on the part of the person to be baptized. They state that the meaning, efficacy and necessity of baptism are to be understood only in the light of the salvation events, and that beyond the rite and its administration, beyond the attitude of the baptized, beyond his faith and repentance and growth in grace, the nature and purpose of God is revealed in the historical salvation events to which the rite of baptism testifies.[1]

It is in the final section of the Report[2] that the nature of faith is most fully dealt with. Three kinds of faith, it is claimed, are to be found in the New Testament, although in full faith the three aspects are not separable. First, intellectual conviction; second, confidence or trust in a person; third, a quality of character which disposes us to a complete trust in God through Christ. The first of these aspects is obviously present where the candidate for baptism is an adult, though everyone who has been baptized on profession of such faith will admit subsequently that at the moment of his baptism his understanding was only partial. It is a mistake therefore to think of the meaning of baptism as being limited to what happens to a person in the baptismal act, and no baptism is complete until a person has received his resurrection body. Whilst it is admitted that Paedo-Baptists need to pay more attention to the place given in the New Testament to the faith of the recipient, it is also pointed out that the attitude of the recipient and what happens in the moment of baptism are not the only factors to be considered. The faithfulness of God in Christ is of primary concern.

Important also is the faith of the congregation, which is compared to the attitude of faith that accompanied some of our Lord's miracles, and the faith of the parents or sponsors which alone can ensure that the child hears the Word and has the opportunity to assent to it in faith.

As a result of all these aspects of faith the child himself may come one day to be aware of faith and to respond to it, and the Report concludes by asserting that it is just as impossible to distinguish between the act of God and the

[1] *Op. cit.*, 14-15.   [2] *Op. cit.*, 55 ff.

act of man in the sacraments as it is to distinguish clearly between the human and the divine in the life of Jesus.

Part II of the Report makes it even more clear that the men who are behind it stand in the Reformed tradition, and any who suspect them of "magic water" and *ex opere operato* teaching should read this section with care.[1] There is on the contrary a warning against false doctrines of baptismal regeneration due to the loss of the historical emphasis on Christ's birth and resurrection for us, and of the eschatological perspective of the ultimate regeneration. There is also criticism of that conception of baptism which sees it as a kind of "prophylactic" protection against disease and the power of evil spirits, said to be due to the early influence of Hellenism. One of the chief criticisms made of the post-apostolic period as a whole is of that conception of grace, mechanically infused, on which the Roman idea of merit is built, and which necessitated the Reformation, for it is openly acknowledged that the *ex opere operato* view of the sacraments is a heresy to the reformed Church.

The emphasis on faith is maintained in this section and it is stated that in the early Church baptism was the chief occasion for instruction and was set in the context of the preaching of the gospel and the teaching of the Word of God.

At times it is difficult in all this not to feel that what the writers really have in mind is believers' baptism, and that it is only by special pleading that their scholarship can be applied to infant baptism. Nevertheless there is developing here a new emphasis on faith and repentance within a Paedo-Baptist community, and if we are to build a solid theology of baptism within the ecumenical context it is one we cannot afford to ignore.

Similar tendencies are to be found within Anglicanism and by no means only among evangelicals. According to E. J. Bicknell,[2] baptism is a sign of regeneration or new birth whereby a man is grafted into the Church and the

[1] Cf. my article in the *Baptist Times*, May 30, 1957.
[2] *Op. cit.*, 463.

promises of the forgiveness of sins and of his adoption to be a son of God are visibly signed and sealed. In scripture it signified the public acknowledgment of Jesus as Lord[1] and is concerned with adults.[2] The language of the Prayer Book also suggests that it belongs in its full sense only to adults and requires accommodation to the new conditions when it is applied to infants. Whilst he tacitly accepts such accommodation as right and inevitable, however, he does also make it crystal clear that faith and repentance are necessary conditions where they can be had.[3]

Since 1940 many discussions of the rite have been taking place within the Church of England[4] and in 1948 an important theological commission appointed by the Archbishops to consider the relation of baptism, confirmation and holy communion declared[5] that justification is by faith and that baptism is the sign and seal of the justifying grace of God, whereby the redeemed sinner becomes the child of God. The baptism of infants is defended on the grounds that where the parents are Christian it is congruous with the doctrine of the Church as a spiritual family and declares the priority of God's act in the salvation and sanctification of his people. Faith and repentance are not overlooked in this instance but are rather regarded as being guaranteed by the sponsors. Such an interpretation should also be approached in the light of A. E. J. Rawlinson's comment[6] that in the early Church of New Testament days Christian initiation meant forgiveness of sins and cleansing, the gift of the spirit, sonship to God and the entry upon a wholly new kind of life; all were associated with baptism. In other words, when the Anglicans speak of baptism they often mean the whole process of Christian initiation, occupying in many instances a period of years, and not simply an act in water.

[1] *Ibid.*, 466.　　　　　[2] *Ibid.*, 473.
[3] *Ibid.*, 474.
[4] For a summary see E. A. Payne, "Baptism in Recent Discussion", in A. Gilmore (ed.), *Christian Baptism*, 18 f.
[5] *The Theology of Christian Initiation*, 16, 22.
[6] *Christian Initiation*, 7. Cf. C. F. D. Moule, "Baptism with Water and Baptism with the Holy Ghost", in *Theology*, 48 (1945), 247–8.

It is hardly surprising therefore that much discussion has gone on within Anglicanism as to the relationship between baptism and confirmation. Some scholars[1] have called for the abandonment of infant baptism and a return to adult baptism, which would make the act of initiation a single unified act and would lead to the revival of the scriptural connection between baptism and a conscious response. Others[2] have tried to see confirmation as a strengthening of what was given in baptism and as the occasion where faith is most relevant, and it has even been asserted that it is to the rite of confirmation that most of the New Testament phrases about baptism and faith really apply. This is the viewpoint which finds most favour with G. W. H. Lampe after his careful survey of the subject.[3] As a result of the stress on faith and confirmation, he says, there has been laid an increasing emphasis on its catechetical rather than its sacramental character, and it now comprises the candidate's public profession of faith, completing his baptism by the addition to it of what had been an essential part of the adult baptism of the early church.

Some members of the Anglican communion have even gone so far as to lay all the emphasis on confirmation, regarding baptism as little more than a preliminary to this great sacrament. Dix adopted the line that infant baptism is always abnormal and needs the response of faith for its completion. K. E. Kirk, similarly, pleaded for baptism and confirmation together when years of discretion had arrived, and although it is true that this led to a sacramental emphasis on confirmation which is quite foreign to Baptists, and, one may even feel, to certain other erroneous conclusions,[4] it

[1] This point of view is reflected in *Baptism Today* (1949), the schedule attached to the second interim report of the Joint Committees on Baptism, Confirmation and Holy Communion.

[2] C. F. D. Moule, *loc. cit.*, 249: A. M. Ramsey, "The Doctrine of Confirmation", in *Theology*, 48 (1945), 194–201.

[3] *The Seal of the Spirit*, 313.

[4] K. E. Kirk and others, for instance, have even tried to argue from this that a baptized and unconfirmed Christian has not received the Holy Spirit sacramentally, and A. M. Ramsey has argued that in the

will be clear that the motive behind it was a desire to link baptism more closely with faith and repentance.

All these discussions have now been focused in the most recent Anglican statement on the subject, *Baptism and Confirmation*.[1] This sets out proposals for the revision of the baptismal services, and the Introduction states that in drafting the services the chief concern of the Commission has been "to relate the pouring of the water to the making of the act of faith".[2] It also makes clear that it believes adult baptism to have been the norm in the New Testament, and that it is only in the light of this fact that the doctrine and practice of baptism can be understood.

It is then further claimed that in early times the two were simultaneous, the act of faith constituting the "form" of the sacrament, of which the water constituted the "matter", the two being separated for the first time in 1552.

When the members of the Commission sought to put this into practice in designing the services, they adopted the line of regarding the baptism of adults as the norm and therefore of putting it first. Prior to his baptism the candidate must renounce the devil, the world and the flesh, and must declare his belief in the Trinity and his willingness to obey the one in whom he believes.

All this must commend itself as a valiant attempt on the part of Anglican scholars and pastors to re-establish the link between faith and baptism. What happens, however, when they come, as ultimately they must, to infant baptism? Two things. First, they cut out the passage where our Lord takes little children into his arms and blesses them (Mark 10: 13–16), on the ground that this passage has no obvious connection with baptism, and substitute for it the Lord's command to baptize all nations (Matt. 28: 18–20).

undivided rite of initiation in the early Church it was through confirmation rather than baptism that the Holy Spirit was mediated. This position has been criticized by R. H. Fuller, "Baptism and Confirmation", in *Theology*, 49 (1946), 113–18.

[1] A Report submitted by the Church of England Liturgical Commission to the Archbishops of Canterbury and York, 1958.

[2] *Op. cit.*, x.

Secondly, they make it quite clear that the questions are to be put to the child and not to the god-parents. This is perfectly in line with the 1662 and 1928 Prayer Books and it is a misconception of the Promises which sees them as statements made by the god-parents about themselves, but this recommended revision improves on the third question (Will you therefore obey him in whom you have believed?) in that it invites obedience to a living Being rather than to the less personal expression of that Being in "his holy will and commandments".[1] E. C. Whitaker,[2] who discusses these changes in some detail, admits that many people feel an element of artificiality about sponsors answering for babies, but defends the practice on the grounds that the primary concern of the Church in baptism is with the faith of the candidate, "no matter whether he is an adult or an infant, no matter whether his faith is a present reality or a hope for the future". If we are to seek for an expression of the god-parents' faith, then we must find some other place in the rite for it.

When we go a step further and ask what is meant by faith in this context we need to turn to the Promises for the answer. There it is quite clear that it includes three things; it is a deliberate turning away from evil, it is an intellectual acceptance of certain credal assertions about the Trinity, and it is a solemn commitment of oneself to a Person. We may question how all this can be properly related to an infant, but we have no right to question the Anglican connection between faith and baptism or the claim that what the Anglican understands by faith is basically very similar to what the Baptist understands by faith.

One of the last places where most British Protestants would expect to find this link between faith and baptism is in the Church of Rome, and for that reason too many would not even look for it. Because of the nature of the Church of Rome it must be admitted that it is not so easy to see and to

[1] Cf. E. C. Whitaker, *The Proposed Services of Baptism and Confirmation Reconsidered*, 18.
[2] *Ibid.*

estimate changes that are taking place as it is elsewhere, though the recent Vatican Council has turned out to be an excellent window opening out on to the world. Nevertheless it is possible to see this emphasis, particularly in some of the more recent Roman Catholic works. For purposes of illustration we will select two which may be regarded as typical of others.

In dealing with the general question of the efficacy of the sacraments, B. Leeming[1] says that all Christians agree that in the case of adults fruitful reception of sacraments requires faith; where Catholics and Protestants differ is only in the particular part that faith plays. He goes on to point out, however, that it is a misconception of Catholic doctrine to say that repentance and living faith are not required in the recipient of the sacrament, and he firmly rejects the view that an *ex opere operato* doctrine implies an excessively materialistic outlook upon the divine power as if it could be localized in material elements. He rejects also the notion that faith in sacramental efficacy is nothing but belief in magic, and he compares magic and the sacraments at some length in order to prove his point.

The other book is a more specific biblical study, dealing with Pauline mysticism,[2] of which one chapter is devoted to "The Means of Union with Christ". Wikenhauser begins by showing the weaknesses of the traditionally Protestant doctrine that union with Christ is brought about by faith which, he alleges, fails to do justice to the objective side of Paul's mysticism; instead he asserts that this objective relationship is brought about by baptism. Such a view does not exclude faith, however, for faith accompanies union with Christ.

He then asks what is meant by faith in Paul's teaching and says that when Paul speaks of faith he means the agreement of the intellect with the content of the gospel message; in other words, the voluntary acceptance of the message of salvation as divine truth. Thus faith entails obedient

[1] *Principles of Sacramental Theology*, 78 ff.
[2] A. Wikenhauser, *Pauline Mysticism*.

subjection of oneself to the gospel as to a binding rule of conduct. In this sense faith may be regarded as the indispensable preliminary before a man can be admitted to baptism, and (still in this sense) it must of necessity lead to baptism, so that just as it is legitimate to say, "No baptism without faith", it is also legitimate to say, "No (genuine) faith without baptism".

Faith, taken in this sense, is therefore initially something intellectual, an acceptance of the message of salvation which God had wrought in Christ. Ultimately, however, it has an ethical content in that it leads to a certain way of life. It is true that it is not of itself the means whereby a man becomes one with Christ, since this union is established by baptism, but it is nevertheless very closely bound up with it and since it does in fact precede and follow the act of baptism it would be impossible to argue that it is unrelated to it.

In this case, as in all the other cases quoted, what one reads in the writings of the more advanced denominational thinkers may not necessarily accord with what the local representatives acclaim, nor directly with the official Canons of the Church. It is nevertheless to such people that we must learn to listen, and when we survey the way we have come two points of fairly general agreement emerge.

First, whilst the faith that is linked with baptism may on occasions be the faith of the congregation or the faith of the sponsors, in nearly every case it is recognized also that there must be faith on the part of the candidate himself. Secondly, whilst there is no clearly consistent understanding of what is meant by faith, it does normally include a response to what God has done in Christ and it often has both intellectual and ethical considerations.

If then this new emphasis on the close relationships between faith and baptism is as real and as genuine as it appears, and if it is to be found in the early reformers, in the new biblical scholarship, in continental theology, in the Church of Scotland, the Church of England, and even in Rome, then one place where we should expect to find this working out in a practical way is in the various schemes of Church union that have marked the life of the younger Churches in recent years. And we do not look in vain.

In the case of the united church of South India there is still a good deal of variety since there has been no attempt to impose uniformity in worship but rather to have variety, and all the orders of worship in use in the uniting Churches before union are still permissible in the united Church. The Liturgy Committee of the Church of South India, however, has produced *An Order for Holy Baptism*[1] which has been authorized by the Executive Committee of the Synod "for optional and experimental use wherever it is desired". Its roots are to be found in the Book of Common Prayer, but its final form represents the impact of the different heritages upon each other. T. S. Garrett,[2] who has been involved in the work of compilation, claims that the work also represents a return to the great tradition of the ancient liturgies which in turn have been submitted to the insights of the Reformation and to modern liturgical study.

These compilers have taken the view that baptism really does confer a spiritual gift and status, thereby excluding the concept of the sacrament as only a symbolic declaration of what the candidate already is receiving apart from it. At the same time they have dissociated themselves from a presentation that would so stress the divine operation in the sacraments as to give less than due place to the response of faith in making the divine gift effective. "But", writes T. S. Garrett,[3] "within these bounds there is room for movement and growth in our understanding."

Because of this desire it is not possible to say exactly what is understood by faith in this Order; its meaning will emerge into clarity as the years pass, but already it is clear that the broad approach of South India is in line with the conclusions we have reached.

[1] Oxford University Press, 1954.
[2] "Baptism in the Church of South India", in *S.J.Th.*, 8 (1955), 385–91.
[3] *Ibid.*

In the scheme for Church union in Ceylon it has been agreed that confession of personal faith in Jesus Christ must be a factor in the process of Christian initiation, and it is stated that the grace of Christ conferred in baptism is appropriated into salvation by repentance and faith. Witness before the congregation of the candidate's belief in Jesus Christ as Saviour and Lord is therefore a very important section in the full service of initiation, a process which is not regarded as complete until the initiate participates for the first time in holy communion.[1]

The same feature is to be found in the *Plan of Church Union in North India and Pakistan*,[2] where in the case of those baptized in infancy it is declared that before such candidates are admitted to the communicant membership of the church they shall give evidence of repentance, faith and love towards Jesus Christ, and in making this public profession of faith they are recognizing their baptism as the outward visible sign of the regenerating grace of God.

From this survey of the links between faith and baptism, it is clear that there are many aspects of faith and baptism on which all Christians are agreed. These include the element of faith and prayer within the congregation; the idea that faith includes intellectual conviction, a response to a Person and a quality of character which reveals a trust in God through Christ; the connection between baptism and instruction and between baptism and the preaching of the Word: and the idea that baptism is only the beginning in the sense that it is the first sign of a man's response to God.

Equally, however, other aspects of the link between faith and baptism make us pause and ask questions. When people speak of no baptism without faith, have they clearly understood what is meant by faith, and is their understanding adequate to the full meaning of the term? In the Baptist emphasis on baptism, has sufficient attention been paid to

[1] R. C. Cowling, "Church Union in Ceylon", in *Missionary Herald*, November 1955, 170–1.
[2] See Third Revised Edition, 1957, 5–7.

the series of salvation events which lies behind the ceremony, and have Baptists been wholly true to their emphasis on the priority of scripture when they have tended to limit their interpretation of baptism to an act of immersion instead of interpreting fully what *baptisma* really means in the New Testament?

Other aspects of the sacramental life, it would appear, have eluded Baptists and evangelicals in other branches of the Church, in whole or in part, and fresh thinking is needed to complete our understanding. They have not always seen, for instance, how the sacraments can deliver them from a purely spiritual religion and enable them to relate their worship to life; too often in fact they have not even wanted it to be too closely so related.[1] And although Baptists have never thought of baptism apart from preaching, they have never really given enough attention to the precise link between Word and sacrament, seen for instance against the background of the prophetic word and the prophetic act, and are still reluctant to acknowledge that infant baptism is not necessarily a magical belief in baptismal regeneration.

To some of these issues we shall return in due course. Meanwhile, two general points need to be made. First, all Christians would do well to acquire for themselves a new charity and a new willingness to listen to what other people are thinking and feeling. We must resist the temptation to attack what other people used to say, or what we think they are saying, or maybe even what on the basis of their historical and doctrinal position we think they ought to be saying, as well as the tendency to retire into the bastions of our history and, like a dog in a manger, refuse to move. Instead let Christians cultivate again their conception of the Lord of Truth, coupled with a new willingness to follow where he may choose to lead.

Secondly, each section of the Church needs to deepen its

[1] The kind of argument advanced, for instance, by J. A. T. Robinson, would be foreign to most Baptists, some of whom would not even want to accept it. (*On Being the Church in the World*, 31–71, especially 58–71.)

own theology of baptism. Practice must then be reformed according to theology. But before we can do that there is another major issue on which some clarification of thought is necessary; it is the relationship between the spiritual, the material and the sacramental.

3

THE MATERIAL, THE SPIRITUAL
AND THE SACRAMENTAL

THE relationship between the material world and the spiritual world, particularly with regard to the sacraments, causes much discussion, and words like "effect" and "efficacy" very quickly become charged with emotional content. By tradition, Baptists have been brought up to believe that the connection between the material world and the spiritual world, if indeed there is any connection, is slight.

It is not surprising, therefore, that for them, the traditional attitude to the sacraments has been largely one of indifference, if not opposition. There is, for instance, a strong body of older Baptist opinion which rejects the word "sacrament" and clings to the word "ordinance", and even where the word "sacrament" has been accepted it is only in a few places that the full content of the word has been appreciated. Baptism is seen often as simply a nailing of one's colours to the mast in the sense that it is a public profession of faith, and the stress has fallen mainly on what a candidate is doing for God in his heart, and not on what he is doing with his body, nor with what God has done for him. The Lord's Supper has been seen similarly as a memorial meal when man remembers what God has done for him on the cross, and re-dedicates himself to his master; and not as an occasion when God re-creates the life that is in him.

During the last couple of decades, however, the ecumenical movement has forced every branch of the Church to listen to the others. This, coupled with a new emphasis on sacramental theology, has led a body of younger Baptist opinion to see how far Baptist thinking is in need of amendment in the light of new truth.

At the outset it must be admitted that much of the interest which Baptists have shown has been of a defensive nature.

The doubts and suspicions cast on infant baptism by scholars like Barth and Brunner were greeted with enthusiasm, as also were some of the writings and arguments of F. J. Leenhardt, in so much that on at least one occasion E. A. Payne[1] had to remind the denomination that they must not think that their case had been universally conceded, for outspoken as these scholars have been in regard to their own Church's theory and practice, they do not become Baptists. On the other hand, the writings of Cullmann and of some members of the Church of Scotland have tended to be dismissed as being misguided rather than unauthentic.

Behind this self-defence there obviously lies a fear. It is the fear that Catholic and sacramentarian teaching might be accepted by the growing generation of Baptists. It is more than that: it is the fear that some Baptists might run away with the idea that in the sacraments something happens. It is more even that that: deep down, it is the fear that in the sacraments God might *do* something. After asking whether anything happens in baptism, R. L. Child[2] (himself a Baptist) replies, "Some good Baptists apparently think not. Indeed, at times, they almost give us the impression that they rather hope not too. . . ."

Baptists therefore must make up their minds on two major issues. First, whether they really want to have anything to do with sacraments at all. It would, of course, be a strange denomination without baptism, but the lengths to which some Baptists will go in order to prove that in baptism nothing happens,[3] coupled with the loose attitude to baptism in many Baptist churches (whereby baptism may be administered with or without membership, before or after membership, or not at all) all seem to indicate that the logical place for such people to be is with the Friends, or the Salvation Army. Clearly, for them, the rite is not of such importance

[1] *The Doctrine of Baptism*, 7.

[2] "What Happens in Baptism", in *Baptist Times*, February 4, 1960.

[3] Many of these writers have forgotten a comment from the Baptist reply to Lambeth, 1926, "Christian Baptism and the Lord's Supper are duly received by us not only as rites instituted by our Lord Himself but as means of grace to all who receive them in faith."

as to justify their existence as a separate denomination. Yet despite the fact that the majority of Baptists must come in this category one cannot resist the feeling that if a decision were to be made the vote would go heavily in favour of some sacramental life.

That would then pin-point the second issue. If Baptists are to retain the sacraments then Baptists must be prepared to produce a theology of the sacraments. And in producing such a theology they must be prepared to consider what other branches of the Church, including Rome and Canterbury, think and believe about the sacraments. They must be prepared also to go to the Bible with an open mind.

Here are two typical examples of the traditionally Baptist way of looking at the relationship between the spiritual and the material.

The first is found in *What Baptists Stand For*.[1] Henry Cook almost goes out of his way to distinguish between the spiritual and the material. The Romanists, with their doctrine of transubstantiation, and the Lutherans, with their doctrine of consubstantiation, are accused of "trying to materialize something that is and must be essentially spiritual", whilst great care is taken to make plain that the water and the bread and the wine are "merely symbolic".

The second example is found in *The Lord's Supper: a Baptist Statement*,[2] quoting a statement made by the Baptist Union Council in 1948. Whilst recognizing the two sacraments, the Council felt obliged to insert this sentence: "We hold that . . . Christ is really and truly present, *not in the material elements*, but in the heart and mind and soul of the believer." (Italics mine.)

What we want to ask is whether in the light of modern scholarship it is both right and profitable to keep trying to drive this wedge between the spiritual world and the material world. Let us look briefly at some of the recent developments in the realms of science, medicine and psychiatry before proceeding to examine recent biblical scholarship.

[1] 1947 edition, pp. 71–72.   [2] pp. 8–9.

1. *Science, Medicine and Psychiatry*

Much recent scientific scholarship is not nearly so sure of the rigid distinction between matter and spirit as were the scientists of some fifty years ago. C. A. Coulson[1] has demonstrated this point in some detail to show that whereas fifty years ago it was firmly believed that science was concerned with the material world only, science today is regarded by many as an essentially religious activity. Facts are never fully known and can never be completely correlated, with the result that question marks are now being placed against many of the old so-called "certainties". The observer cannot be independent of the thing he observes, and the scientist who limits himself to the facts misses some of the glory just as much as does the Christian who thinks that Christianity is nothing more than an acceptance of the Creed, whilst science itself cannot exist without judgments of value, without certain attitudes of heart and mind, and even without moral convictions, which are none the less imperative because they go unrecognized.

The significance of such an estimate can be appreciated the more readily if one turns to literature on science and religion dating from the beginning of the century.[2] The kind of arguments used reveals days when men believed science and religion to be antagonistic the one to the other, and those who wanted to believe set themselves to show that such an attitude was mistaken.[3] They were the days when men were saying that science could satisfy the needs of man and that religion was superfluous, and those who were men of faith again set themselves to prove the weakness of the argument.[4] They were days when the only satisfactory

[1] *Science and Christian Belief*, 43 ff., 54 ff.

[2] e.g. *Science and Religion*, by Seven Men of Science (1914). Lectures given by leading scientists of the day during Science Week, held in Browning Hall, London.

[3] Cf. Edward Hull, "The Witness of Geology to Revelation", in *Science and Religion*, 77 ff.

[4] Cf. W. A. Bottomley, "Religion and the Crowning Stone of Science", in *Science and Religion*, 59 ff.

solution seemed to be that which saw science and religion not as opposed but as allies: two great departments of one vast domain. But they were still essentially *two* departments. The one was the outer court where the student could trace out the laws of nature; the other was an inner shrine in which the soul of man could find the assurance of an over-ruling power. Those who saw that faith was essential to scientific research were few and far between,[1] and even some of those who did plead that the two ways of looking at the universe should not be kept in water-tight compart-ments seemed more anxious that religion should accept the facts of scientific enquiry than that science should acknow-ledge its need of religion.[2]

The idea that such a change in scientific thinking has taken place is further fortified by the general change of approach. The older writers were on the defensive, con-cerned to claim as much for religion as was possible and anxious lest they should appear to concede too much ground to the scientist. W. A. Whitehouse[3] says that even comparatively recent works like E. L. Mascall's *Christian Theology and Natural Science*, and Mary Hesse's *Science and the Human Imagination* scarcely do more than give the im-pression that science and faith are two tired old warhorses which it is profitless to parade in contests for public approval; the stage has now been reached when each can go its own way without help or hindrance from the other, whilst the well-informed person can, if he wants to, drive them as a pair without falling into a ditch. The dangers of this division are described today by J. S. Habgood[4] as "an uneasy truce" and he goes on to focus attention on the seriousness of this division both for science and for religion.

Whitehouse further criticizes[5] the habit of trying to build

[1] Cf. J. A. Fleming, "The Supreme Intelligence in and above Nature", in *Science and Religion*, 31 ff.

[2] Cf. J. Arthur Thomson, *Science and Religion*, 22 ff.

[3] *Order, Goodness, Glory*, 3.

[4] "The Uneasy Truce Between Science and Religion", in A. R. Vidler (ed.), *Soundings*, 23 ff.

[5] *Op. cit.*, 8.

bridges between the positive results of science and the theory and practice of religion, on the grounds that such methods are now out of fashion. Nowadays a writer is able to assume the interdependence of one on the other, and from that to consider such fundamental questions as the structure of knowledge and the basis of ethics, and to look for a theology which is of some use in our present situation without committing scientists to quasi-religious motives or suppositions.[1]

What we have said is sufficient to indicate a change in scientific thought. To the scientist the worlds of matter and spirit are not nearly so clearly distinguished the one from the other as used to be imagined. We may now go on to see how the same barrier has been broken down in the field of medicine and psychiatry.

David Stafford-Clark,[2] in discussing the place of psychiatry in modern medicine, says that today the old dichotomy of mind and spirit has at least begun finally to be resolved by an acceptance of the interdependence of the one upon the other. Doctors, he says, have known for years that anxious, worried or miserable patients heal slowly and relapse often, and the way medicine has been studied in the twentieth century was bound to lead them to recognize more and more contributory factors which played their part in varying degree in the course of any particular illness. The same period has seen a similar development in the study of the mind, and thus the way was paved for the integration of psychiatry and general medicine, when physical illness could be studied from a psychiatric standpoint and psychiatric illness could be studied from the point of view of physical change. Thus has been built up a body of knowledge which it is fashionable to refer to as psychosomatic medicine, but it is most important to recognize that this does not refer to any particular disease or group of illnesses, still less to a particular speciality in medicine open only to a particular

[1] Cf. J. A. T. Robinson's attempts to deal with the subjects of Matter, Power and Liturgy in *On Being the Church in the World*, 31 ff.
[2] *Psychiatry To-day*, 232 ff.

kind of doctor. It is in fact a method of approach which no good doctor ignores, based upon an acceptance of the body-mind relationship and all it implies.

That there is more to this than simply the body and the mind is admitted later by the same writer[1] when he says that even after complete and successful analysis the subject has still no more than his own individual human resources on which to rely, and these are not always enough. Sometimes the conflicts of which the subject becomes aware remain insoluble for him. The patient, groping beyond himself for the final answer, cannot get it from the analyst. To this question the psychiatrist *qua* psychiatrist has no answer. David Stafford-Clark simply comments, ". . . as a man I can only say with all humility that I believe in God". The psychiatrist may have no answer but few psychiatrists would want to claim that the problems with which they deal are in a class totally apart from those which are the concern of the parish priest.

The dawning of this realization during the present century has not surprisingly therefore led to closer co-operation between doctors and ministers of religion. In 1910 a conference of priests and doctors was called to consider the possibilities of closer co-operation in the treatment of the sick. In 1930 the Lambeth Conference was able to plead for a growing co-operation between doctors and clergy on the grounds of "the constant inter-relation of body and spirit"[2] and to welcome the existence of a permanent committee of clergy and doctors to deal with spiritual healing.

It is true that the place accorded to the spirit in the day-to-day work of the general practitioner may not be all that some would wish, but nevertheless it is undeniable that the climate has changed.

Modern psychology, and a study of the unconscious and the subconscious, also has something to say on this point, particularly with regard to symbols.

[1] *Op. cit.*, 286 ff.
[2] For a full survey of these movements towards co-operation, see "Priest-Doctor", *Christus Integritas*, 9 ff.

A child's sense of security depends on the fact not simply that he is loved, but that he feels he is loved; he must be caressed. And it is futile to argue that a caress is so many pounds of pressure being exerted on a child's trunk by his parents' arms,[1] as if it could be done as well by a machine, for we all know that there is something in that caress that sums up a whole attitude and approach, that defies description and analysis but which has its effect upon the child.

And in the same way it is wrong to treat the sacraments purely on a rational level in order to show how meaningless they are, for they are not given simply for man's mental powers, but for the whole man.

The broad picture has been admirably summarized by Amos N. Wilder[2] who writes, "The whole trend of our age is against dividing man up into body and soul, and dividing his values up into material and spiritual. Whether we look at psychology, philosophy or aesthetics, we find a common repudiation of this severing of flesh and spirit, and theology today joins the chorus." That being the case the theologian can never afford to cut himself off from other fields of knowledge in order to maintain the *status quo* within his own field, and it is particularly wrong if he of all people continually strives to make divisions where other people no longer find them. It is perhaps significant, therefore, that where the theologian's ears have been wide open, the closing of the gap between the material and the spiritual worlds has also had its effects in ecclesiastical circles, and has revealed itself in an increasing appreciation of the sacraments.

P. T. Forsyth's[3] comment that within the Free Churches there was a feeling that they had not yet entered into their sacramental heritage, and that to that extent their spiritual life had been beggared and impoverished, must have raised

---

[1] "The act of fondling, the kiss, the embrace, are not employed for the purpose of leaving direct impressions upon the infant's body: rather they are expressions of feeling or at least are actions symbolic of human feeling." (F. W. Dillistone, *Christianity and Symbolism*, 174.)

[2] *New Testament Faith for Today*, 21 f.

[3] *The Church and the Sacraments*, 166.

many an eyebrow in 1917; today there can be no doubt that throughout the whole of the Church this increasing appreciation of the sacraments is apparent. The growth of the liturgical movement everywhere is an indication of the way things are going.

There is, however, one vital difference between these movements in the Church and elsewhere. Elsewhere, the developments are accepted, though with somewhat varying degrees of enthusiasm; within the Church, there is a conservatism that dies hard. The result tends to be an amassing of the forces on either side: those who are determined to stick to the old traditional answers and arguments, indifferent to the fact that some of them no longer apply, *versus* those who are equally determined to move forward with what they at any rate consider to be progress. Such a situation is regrettable in that it can lead only to deadlock, division and wounds in the body of Christ. It is better that we should look at such issues together with an open mind to try to see how they have come about.

2. *Biblical Theology*

To do this we must now turn from modern scholarship in general to modern biblical theology, looking first at the new approach that has come about in the field of Old Testament scholarship to the relationship between the priest and the prophet. "A generation or two ago," writes S. C. Carpenter,[1] "Old Testament scholars were accustomed to find, as a matter of course, an acute cleavage between priest and prophet. The priest stood for the performance, often rather mechanical, of ceremonial usages, and the prophet broke in upon his barren conventions with the Sword of the Spirit." And those who went through a theological college before about 1925 will remember this well.

On the surface there is much evidence to support it. Some passages in the writings of the prophets appear positively hostile to the cult and to the temple;[2] some psalms seem to

[1] *Priest and Prophet*, 3.
[2] Cf. H. H. Rowley, *The Unity of the Bible*, 30–33.

belong to the temple liturgy and some seem indifferent to sacrifice; what better then than to say that some came from the priestly school and some came from the prophetic school? Once the theory had been adopted, evidence that pointed in the opposite direction was often summarily dismissed. Of the organized associations of prophets that existed in connection with the cultus in pre-exilic times, and their favourable reactions towards it, for example, O. Eissfeldt[1] says the old answer was that this applied only to the popular prophets, and not to the reform or writing prophets. As for the interest which post-exilic prophets showed in sacrifice and in the observances of the cultus, it was always asserted that those men really belonged to the priestly classes in their approach, that their message was different from that of their pre-exilic counterparts, and that this was in part the cause of the decline of religion in the post-exilic period. Josiah's Law-book, on the other hand, was held to be so much in the prophetic strain that its composition was normally attributed to the seventh century and its teaching was held to spring from the work of the eighth-century prophets.

Such distinctions played into the hands of the ecclesiastics. Those who were reared in nonconformity, and whose parents had been struck by the rise and growth of the Oxford Movement, firmly believed that they represented the prophetic wing and went out of their way to show up the dangers of the priestly concept of religion as witnessed in the Bible as well as in their own experience. Those who had been born into institutionalism, on the other hand, accused the nonconformists of neglecting half of the biblical revelation and defended themselves on the basis of the post-exilic period and the letter to the Hebrews.

In some circles these answers are still being given, but they are less powerful today than ever they were, because modern biblical scholarship has come to see a unity in the priest-prophet controversy. H. H. Rowley[2] even suggests that this

---

[1] "The Prophetic Literature", in H. H. Rowley (ed.), *The Old Testament and Modern Study* (1951 edition), 119.

[2] *The Unity of the Bible*, 36. Cf. S. C. Carpenter, *op. cit.*, 4.

division between priest and prophet was a contemporary issue that was read back into biblical times.

Space does not permit us to deal with all the arguments, which can be found in full in other places,[1] but today there is an increasing number of scholars who feel that the old dichotomy between two types of Old Testament religion, the one priestly and ritualistic, the other prophetic and ethical, can no longer be sustained; the legal and the prophetic portions of the Old Testament are not in fact so completely at cross-purposes.[2] The prophetic books in their present form come from the post-exilic period, which is unlikely if their approach to the faith were so vastly different. The formation of the canon was a post-exilic process, and again it is unlikely that both elements would have been included if they had been thought to be fundamentally opposed to each other.[3] Moreover, many of the crucial texts are now seen to be capable of alternative interpretations.[4]

If we turn next to the Law, there is not now believed to be any evidence for the idea that so long as men offer the right sacrifices they may live how they please. H. H. Rowley[5] shows how the decalogue, the covenant, Deuteronomy and the Code of Holiness all plead for obedience and contain nothing of which the greatest prophets need have been ashamed.

The conclusion of modern scholarship, therefore, is that the prophets were not opposed to ritual *qua* ritual. They were only opposed to ritual that was not the organ of the spirit. When they pleaded "not sacrifice but obedience" they were concerned with priorities rather than alternatives, and

[1] Cf. N. W. Porteous, "Prophet and Priest in Israel", in *Expository Times*, lxii (1950–51), 4 ff.: O. Eissfeldt, "The Prophetic Literature", in H. H. Rowley (ed.), *The Old Testament and Modern Study* (1951 edition) 115 ff.

[2] H. H. Rowley, *The Unity of the Bible*, 33 ff.

[3] S. C. Carpenter (*op. cit.*, 4) says it would be like supposing that the Elizabethan Marprelate Tracts had been included, with the Thirty-Nine Articles, as an appendix to the Book of Common Prayer.

[4] Cf. H. H. Rowley, *ibid.*   [5] *Ibid.*

were declaring that for lack of obedience sacrifice was being invalidated.[1] And this is surely not without its significance for the modern ecclesiastical debate. It means that the old distinction between the ritual and the ethical, and between the spiritual and the institutional, can no longer be sustained on the evidence of the Old Testament. Indeed, it means more; it means that the Old Testament clearly teaches the use of the material as the organ of the spiritual.

In reply to this position it can scarcely be argued that it was abrogated by Jesus and that the New Testament is essentially different. It is true that in the Church the sacrificial system came to an end, but that was not because of enlightened prophetic teaching; it was because of the death of Christ. Indeed Jesus Himself seems to have shared the approach of the Old Testament as we now understand it. Prior to His death, He could hardly have regarded sacrifices as alien to the will of God or He would not have required the cleansed lepers to go and offer sacrifices (Luke 17: 14); He must have seen in the temple worship something that could nurture the spirit of the sincere and the humble and bring near to God those who tried to serve Him, or He would never have resorted there as often as He did; and he must have seen some value in conveying a spiritual sense by material means or He would not have spat on the ground and put clay on the eyes of the blind man (John 9: 6). There is therefore nothing in the teaching of Jesus to countermand the general approach of the Old Testament; what we have rather is a tacit acceptance of it.

What happens when we pass to Paul and the early Church? In the days when Old Testament priest and prophet were held over against each other biblical scholarship claimed also to find a similar dualism here. James and the Jerusalem apostolate were regarded as the lineal descendants of the priesthood, with its emphasis on ritualism and legalism; Paul was the prophet, owning allegiance to nobody save his Lord and laying all the stress on the spiritual over against

[1] R. H. Pfeiffer, *Religion in the Old Testament*, 134. Cf. H. W. Robinson, *Redemption and Revelation*, 250.

the material. More widely, the distinction was regarded as one between the regular and what was spoken of as the "charismatic" ministry.[1] Again, the distinction, if not deliberately contrived by the ecclesiastics, certainly played into their hands. The upholders of institutional religion and the upholders of a spiritual religion lined up on either side, and each drew support from different sections of the New Testament. Such events as the Council of Jerusalem (Acts 15) were held to focus the conflict.

But here too there is much evidence that requires us to think again. We single out two or three recent re-statements of the position. J.-L. Leuba,[2] for instance, has surveyed this field and shown that both institutional and spiritual elements can be found perfectly blended together. He begins by taking the names given to Jesus, some of which are institutional (e.g. Son of David, King of the Jews, Christ, Son of God), and some of which are spiritual (e.g. Son of Man, Lord, Servant). He then goes on to show how the same twin characteristics are to be found, similarly blended, in the apostolate, and he thus breaks down the old distinction between the so-called institutional apostolate of the Twelve and the so-called spiritual apostolate of Paul. The New Testament, he declares, knows no distinction in the apostolic ministry, neither does it exalt one aspect over and above the other. The only difference from the perfect blending of the two ideas as they are found in Christ lies in the fact that in the apostolate they cannot be held together in one person. This was, not surprisingly, the cause of some tension, and it is the tension that is reflected in events like the Council of Jerusalem, but it is only tension, and not conflict. The New Testament, for example, presents the apostolate of the Twelve as an institution, and that of Paul as a "charisma", but both apostolic ministries are nevertheless the work of the one Christ. Paul is willing to go to meet the Twelve in Jerusalem, and they are willing to recognize his ministry,

[1] S. C. Carpenter (*op. cit.*, 5) describes this now as an "illegitimate distinction", as if the regular ministry were not a ministry of grace.
[2] *New Testament Pattern* (London, 1953).

whilst that they shared one common gospel had been pointed out years before both by P. T. Forsyth[1] and C. H. Dodd.[2]

In this way Leuba reaches the conclusion that it was the combination of the institutional ministry of the Twelve and the charismatic ministry of Paul that together made up the apostolic ministry. The New Testament does not allow us to ignore the fact that there were differences between the two, but is careful also to show that there was no contradiction.[3]

F. W. Dillistone,[4] about the same time, examined the same problem from the historical point of view as well as from the biblical one, and came to much the same conclusion. He distinguished the two types of churchmanship by using the words "organic" and "covenantal", and concluded that the only way of avoiding the perils of both was by giving the fullest possible scope to the operations of the covenantal principle within the organic environment. He asserts that both principles are essential for the life and growth of any true society,[5] and any truly united Church must have both.

Lesslie Newbigin[6] reached much the same conclusion after examining three different types of modern churchmanship. First, the congregation of the faithful, who lay stress on faith and sound doctrine, and whose descendants are to be found in Protestant bodies. Secondly, the Body of Christ, concerned with continuity, whose descendants are to be found in Catholic bodies. But then, thirdly, the community of the Holy Spirit, laying stress on the idea that the Church exists wherever the Holy Spirit is present. He then went on to show that there can be no New Testament warrant for separating the Spirit of Christ from the Body of Christ, and reminds both Catholic and Protestant traditions not to forget

[1] *The Principle of Authority*, 140 ff.   [2] *Apostolic Preaching*.

[3] What this means in practice, in terms of loyalty to truth and loyalty to the koinonia, is clearly illustrated by W. A. Visser 't Hooft, *The Pressure of our Common Calling*, 68 f.

[4] *The Structure of the Divine Society* (London, 1951).

[5] "The Church is the Body of Christ; the Church is also the people of the New Covenant. The Church is a Sacramental Organism: it is also a Federal Organisation." (*Op. cit.*, 232.)

[6] *The Household of God* (London, 1953).

that they are only bearers of Christ's commission in so far
as they are anointed with His Spirit.[1]

The most recent and thorough statement of these two
biblical trends is to be found in F. J. Leenhardt's *Two
Biblical Faiths: Protestant and Catholic*.[2] Leenhardt finds in
Abraham and Moses the two main emphases of Protestantism and Catholicism, the one coming down to us through
Paul and the other through Peter. Abraham, Paul and
Protestantism all stress the sovereign God who intervenes at
will by His word and so radically transforms the situation in
which He acts. Moses, Peter and Catholicism, on the other
hand, all stress the "coming down" of the revelation from
heaven to earth, its entering into the continuity of history,
its becoming interwoven with the life of the world and
assuming concrete forms. Modern Protestants and Catholics
have each been content to appeal either to Abraham or
Moses and simply to overlook those aspects of the total
revelation which no longer fitted in with their own pre-
suppositions. In conclusion, Leenhardt is prepared to admit
that he has rather overdrawn his pictures in the interests of
making his point, but nothing is to be lost by this. He then
shows how neither form of spirituality has shown the fruits
that it might have produced because they have developed
unilaterally. Now, each must emerge from its doctrinal and
emotional ghetto in order to explore the spiritual and
theological landscape which previously had been alien to it.

For all these writers, as for many others, there is clearly
no ultimate distinction to be made between things spiritual
and things organic, between the material means and the
power of the spirit. In the New Testament, in history and
in practice, they are complementary modes of thought, to
be regarded by the Church not as an either/or but as a both/
and. It is true that Stephen presents a rather different
picture, but his position was something of an isolated one

[1] For the wider implications of these works, particularly as they
relate to Baptists, see my two articles, "The Spirit and the Institution",
in the *Baptist Times*, September 29 and October 6, 1955.
[2] Lutterworth Press.

in the early Church and there is little evidence that later Christian thinkers were influenced by him.[1]

Once we are able to see these two elements united in the early Church, it is not so easy to argue that Paul's emphasis on faith is a determined attack on the regular ministries, forms and rites of the recognized Church. And so we have seen also of late a tendency to find in Paul an approach to the material (one might almost even say a sacramentalism) which to our forefathers would have seemed quite out of place. P. T. Forsyth,[2] though years ahead of his time, was one of the first to criticize Free Church theologians for ignoring the sacramental elements in Paul, or for assuming that his views accorded with their own, and he quotes several scholars[3] of different persuasions who all find a greater sacramentalism in Paul than had previously been realized. He then adds that if there is any sound basis for this new movement, it is perfectly clear that a very serious problem will be raised for Free Church theology. That was written in 1917. I can see a wry smile across his lips if he were here today.

Modern biblical scholarship finds much of the sacramental in Paul. For instance, in a recent study of Pauline mysticism in which a whole section is devoted to baptism, A. Wikenhauser[4] rejects the popular Protestant view that union with Christ is brought about wholly by faith, for such a view could deprive baptism of its total effect, and reduce it to a mere ceremonial rite; there is, he says, an objective side to this mysticism, and this objective relationship is brought about by the sacrament of baptism. He examines the relevant passages to discover what role, if any, is played by faith in the process, and concludes that though faith does not establish union with Christ, it is the indispensable condition for the establishment of this union. "... without faith there is no union

[1] L. W. Barnard, "Saint Stephen and Early Alexandrian Christianity", in *New Testament Studies*, 7 (1960–61), 31–45.

[2] *Op. cit.*, 153 ff.

[3] e.g. Wernle, Pfleiderer, Kirsopp Lake, Weinel, Feine, Tituis, Heitmuller and Schweitzer. P. T. Forsyth himself also examines the evidence on this point at some length.

[4] *Pauline Mysticism*, 109 ff.

with Christ . . . faith is the necessary condition for receiving baptism, which establishes union with Christ" (p. 129).[1]

One further point. This is the fluidity of thought between the individual and the community, and also between the spiritual and the material, which is now a commonplace of biblical scholarship. H. W. Robinson[2] first gave expression in this country to the idea of corporate personality within the Old Testament, showing how the Hebrew mind moved easily and freely between the individual and the community, and this theory has proved helpful in explaining many of the problems connected with the Isaianic servant songs. He it was, too, who first brought out the significance of the symbolism of the prophets,[3] showing the connection between the symbol and the event symbolized and emphasizing the unity of thought to the Hebrew mind of the word, the symbol and the event.

In the New Testament, the idea of corporate personality is found in the writings of Paul in the way in which his mind moves freely from Christ to the Church and back again to Christ. To be "in Christ" is to be "in the Church" and often it is difficult to say with any degree of certainty which Paul had in mind. Similarly, it is equally difficult to see where Paul distinguishes between the spiritual and the material, because this too is a distinction that he does not draw. Salvation, for Paul, comes neither by faith nor by baptism, but by faith *and* baptism.

It is not easy for a westerner to appreciate these modes of thinking, but two illustrations may take us some way towards an understanding, always remembering that no analogy can be applied in every detail. The nearest we get to corporate personality is when we refer to a nation by its leader: for instance, we speak of de Gaulle when sometimes we literally mean de Gaulle, and when at other times we mean France. The nearest we get to the fluidity of thought between

---

[1] A. Wikenhauser then goes on to explain what is meant by faith, the relevance of which we have already looked at in Chapter 2.

[2] Cf. A. S. Peake (ed.), *The People and the Book*, 353 ff.

[3] *Old Testament Essays* (1927). Cf. "Jewish Antecedents", in A. Gilmore (ed.) *Christian Baptism*, 54 ff., for a fuller study of this subject.

the spiritual and the material is in marriage. A couple are not married immediately they fall in love; but neither do we believe that they are married simply by reciting certain words in church and by giving and receiving of a ring. What makes a marriage is neither love nor commitment, but love *and* commitment.

To sum up. We began by noting, how, in the realms of science, medicine and psychiatry, there has been a tendency to acknowledge a lessening of the tension and a breaking down of the barriers between the spiritual and the material, and we saw that this approach to life had coincided with an increasing interest in the sacraments. We then saw how these changes had been accompanied by a new discovery of unity within the Bible which meant that the old distinctions could no longer be upheld. Now, in conclusion, it is important to realize that all these developments have had some effect on sacramental theology, and in any attempt to produce or to estimate a theology of the sacraments they must be taken into consideration.

On the Free Church side, it has led to a fuller appreciation of the sacraments in so far as they are accompanied by faith and are the organ of the spirit. Younger scholars are less ready to declare the sacraments to be unimportant and incidental, to refer to baptism as a "mere" symbol or a "nailing of one's colours to the mast", and to consider attendance at the Lord's Table as free for all and optional for all.

On the Catholic side, there has been a distinct move away from mechanical theories of grace, from *ex opere operato* doctrines, and from the indifferent attitude to faith that marked an earlier generation. B. Leeming[1] says it is a misconception of Catholic doctrine to say that repentance and living faith are not required in the recipient of the sacrament, and goes on to show how in the sacraments there is a blending of the Word with material things.

These may perhaps be nothing more than straws in the wind but they are nevertheless indications as to which way the wind is blowing.

[1] *Principles of Sacramental Theology*, 85, 404.

4

BAPTISM AND CHURCH MEMBERSHIP

WHAT to most branches of the Church is axiomatic, namely that baptism is initiation to church membership, and that there is no membership without baptism, is by no means axiomatic to the majority of Baptists. This is partly because until the last generation no baptism has been recognized as true baptism other than that of the believer, and partly because outward forms have always been regarded as subsidiary to the main thing, which was the believer's own personal faith and commitment to God.

The extremist in this respect, historically speaking, was John Bunyan, for whom baptism was purely subjective and a means of strengthening the faith which the believer already had. Advocates of this point of view are still with us. For them baptism *may* be administered to those who believe, but *need* not be; where it takes place it may precede membership or follow membership; whilst the Church is to decide whom it is to admit to membership it is clearly not able to decide who is to be baptized, such a decision being left either to the candidate himself, in which case baptism is administered very freely indeed, or to the minister who is to conduct the ceremony. Such a view leads to a rigid segregation of baptism and membership, since it does not necessarily follow that every person who is baptized will in fact become a member of the church, whilst, by allowing for membership widely without baptism, it means also that some people may come forward for baptism long after they have become members.

The fact that this point of view exists with some historical basis, and is also an extreme point of view which (perhaps for that reason) achieves a fair degree of publicity, should not, however, blind us to the fact that it is not the only attitude taken up by Baptists. Nor has it ever been the only attitude. The Somerset Confession of 1656, for instance, following largely the Particular Baptist Confession of 1644, makes it clear that baptism is the means by which the believer is planted in the visible Church and in the Body of Christ. This position also has its advocates in Baptist circles today and there is some evidence that their number and influence are increasing.

If we re-examine these two broad approaches in the light of modern biblical interpretations of the New Testament there seems little doubt that the line taken by Bunyan and his followers has no support to speak of.

The Acts of the Apostles, for instance, shows that baptism was the normal rite of admission to the Christian community, and though in those primitive days it does not appear to have been universal or necessary for salvation, there is no indication that spirit-baptism at any stage superseded water-baptism. By the time we come to the period in the early Church reflected in the fourth gospel, the universality of baptism is assured in a more definite way, and John 3: 5 suggests that entrance into the kingdom of God is impossible except by means of the re-birth in baptism which is both a water-baptism and a bestowal of the spirit.

Such an interpretation of the rite of baptism is also in line with the letters of Paul, who saw baptism as the sacrament of union with Christ. That being the case, baptism also involves union with the Body of Christ, making the believer a living member partaking in the whole. Faith is essential to the act, but faith and baptism should be seen as two sides of the same thing. Was it not Basil of Caesarea, often lauded by Baptists because of his insistence on believers' baptism by immersion, who wrote, "Faith and baptism are two ways of salvation, cognate to one another and inseparable"?

Since the authority of scripture and of the New Testament in particular has always been one of the foundation stones of Baptist principles, and since in the providence of God new light and truth are continually breaking forth from His word, Baptists of all people must beware of ignoring the findings of modern biblical scholarship because those findings happen to conflict with present practice or with the positions adopted by some of their earliest advocates.

Perhaps on the analogy of Christian marriage already cited the first requirement is to stop trying to drive a wedge between matter and spirit by asking whether salvation came by baptism or by faith, and then to make a new effort to realize that it comes by both. The gateway to church membership would then be one that was concerned with *both* faith *and* baptism. Evidence collected by E. A. Payne[1] indicates that this more rigid view was in fact the intention of many of the early open membership Churches, and the declaration made at Edinburgh in 1937,[2] that a united Church would observe the rule that all members of the visible Church are admitted by baptism, may be regarded as a further indication that this is the road for the future if we are to make any sound headway in ecumenical relationships.

At the same time, it cannot be overlooked that the widespread adoption of such a theology would lead to a number of practical points to which Baptists would need to find an answer. Before we begin to examine these practical points, however, we had better say something about the relationship between baptism and communion since these two issues are so closely linked to each other. We can then look at all the practical implications together.

Just as there were some Baptists who saw no necessary connection between baptism and church membership, so also there were those who saw no necessary connection between baptism and communion, and (to make matters more complicated) they were not always the same people.

With such an attitude to baptism as John Bunyan had, it is not surprising that he felt the same exactly about baptism and communion. For him, faith alone was the essential prerequisite for admission to the Lord's Table, a baptism of the spirit and not of water. This is still held by some Baptists, with the result that some partake of the communion without being baptized and without being church members.

[1] *The Fellowship of Believers*, 78 ff.
[2] Cited by E. A. Payne in A. Gilmore (ed.), *Christian Baptism*, 16.

Certain other advocates of the open communion position, however, based their arguments on other grounds. Robert Hall,[1] for instance, who may be regarded as the greatest advocate of the open communion position after Bunyan, based his claim almost entirely on the fact that those who had been baptized in some other way (and not those who had never been baptized at all) should be admitted to the Table. It is sometimes argued that this is because Hall had no more regard for baptism than had Bunyan, and therefore the fact that people had been baptized as infants in another branch of the Church was a thing of nought; so long as they were members "by faith" they must be admitted to communion in Baptist churches. If that is so, it is strange that he does not present the same arguments as Bunyan, but he doesn't. He defends open communion because it is an obligation of brotherly love, because scripture enjoins respectful conduct towards Christians who differ in religious sentiments, and because "Paedo-Baptists are members of the true Church and therefore cannot lawfully be excluded from its communion".[2] Moreover, Joseph Kinghorn, who opposed him, did so on the grounds that the unbaptized could not be admitted to the New Testament Church and therefore the question of their presenting themselves at the Lord's Table just did not arise, and Hall replied that it was surely inconsistent to suppose that an involuntary mistake on this subject (baptism) could be a sufficient bar to communion while it was acknowledged to be none to the participation of future blessedness.

None of this really suggests complete indifference to baptism, and whilst it is too early to suggest that this is an acceptance of infant baptism it is certainly an acceptance of the principle of religious freedom and toleration. Hall and his colleagues had no doubt that their non-Baptist brethren were mistaken, but they were prepared at least to try to believe that what they did with regard to baptism might be right for them.

[1] *The Terms of Communion.*
[2] These arguments are considered first hand by D. M. Himbury in A. Gilmore (ed.), *Christian Baptism*, 293–4.

The issue of open communion turned therefore rather on the *fact* of baptism than the *form* of baptism: those who had been baptized and admitted to full membership of any branch of the Church should not be barred from receiving communion in a Baptist church. This is very different from offering communion to every believer whether he had undergone any form of baptism or not. Nowadays, in the modern ecumenical setting in which we find ourselves, this is certainly the approach to open communion which is finding greatest favour and which is being increasingly felt by many Baptists to be the right one.

Nevertheless, the wide variety of viewpoint that is possible with regard to membership and with regard to communion does make the modern situation somewhat complex. The best summary of the Baptist position in recent years is that by Torsten Bergsten[1] in which he marks out three broad positions:

1. "No" to infant baptism as Christian baptism. Closed communion. This is the rigidly closed communion position of those people who believe baptism to be essential to the life of the Christian church, but who recognize only the baptism of believers.

2. "No" to infant baptism. Open communion. This is the more charitable view of those who still believe in the importance of baptism for the Church but who find it hard to un-church their Christian brethren in other branches of the Church to the point of refusing them admission to the Lord's Table. Thus baptism is not regarded as a prerequisite to the Lord's Supper and a distinction (quite alien to the New Testament) is drawn between those who believe and are baptized and those who believe and sit down to the Lord's Supper.

3. "Yes" and "No" to infant baptism. Ecumenical inter-communion. Bergsten here distinguishes two kinds of infant baptism: the one which is administered in the presence of believing parents and god-parents, and which subsequently

[1] "Baptism and the Church", in *Baptist Quarterly*, xviii (1959–60), 162–71.

leads to faith and the fulfilment of the promises made; the other kind, described as indiscriminate, and independent of whether the person being baptized receives faith and accepts grace or not. To say "Yes" means a conditional acknowledgment of infant baptism to the extent that in the first kind baptism stands at the beginning of a process of engrafting the individual into the fellowship of the church. To say "No" is not to deny the right of the Paedo-Baptist Church to be a Church, but rather to insist that some reformation is called for so as to restore baptism to its rightful place within the life of the church and the individual.

Such an attitude would be typical of very many younger Baptist thinkers and of not a few older members of the Baptist denomination, though the practical implications of adopting this line must not be overlooked.

If the phrases used in our Churches in connection with baptism, church membership and communion arose originally out of theology, it is also true that their frequent use today tends in turn to produce a theology. Therefore Baptists with this viewpoint need to re-examine their position to see whether it still expresses what they want it to express. Two phrases in particular arise.

The first is *believers' baptism*. In view of the tendency towards adult baptism within Anglicanism, it is important first to make clear that adult baptism and believers' baptism are not necessarily the same thing. This has often been stated but has not yet been fully appreciated. The matter of age and maturity has never been a vital factor for Baptists; the matter of conviction and response to the love of God has. Because of Baptist concern for children and young people it has usually turned out that most church members were baptized in their teens, but this must not imply that the teens is the time for baptism. There are those who do not come to baptism until late in life, and in recent years there are those who come to baptism at a much younger age than used to be thought normal. In some American Baptist churches in particular, children are regularly baptized, and although one sometimes questions the wisdom of such a practice, it does nevertheless underline the principle that what matters is conviction rather than maturity.

There is, however, another and more serious objection to this phrase. It is doubtful whether it would have been valid in the early days of Baptist history but it is valid today. It arises from the implication that believers' baptism is the baptism of believers; that is, that one becomes a believer and is then baptized. Such an approach is vulnerable because it seems to make baptism a mere appendage to the making of a believer, and separates faith and baptism, spirit and water, in Christian initiation. The weakness of this kind of segregation we have already referred to on biblical and theological grounds, and what we therefore really mean to express by believers' baptism is not the baptism of believers but the making of believers by baptism. Baptism is not to be regarded as an appendage to a man's becoming a disciple; it is rather a focal point of the initiation experience, which finds its culmination in communion and admission to membership.

The other phrase is the popular invitation *to all who love the Lord Jesus Christ* to partake of communion. If it is assumed that all who love the Lord Jesus Christ are in fact members of His Church, baptized and in faith, then the objection may be withdrawn, but in view of the interpretation which has been put on open membership (namely that baptism is a thing of no consequence) and in view of the interpretation that has been put on open communion (namely that it need not be related to either membership or baptism) this phrase tends to encourage a notion which is not in the best biblical and theological tradition. It may be that this pattern of words was originally an attempt to compromise by making it clear that those who loved Jesus Christ, though they may in fact be members of other branches of his Church, were certainly welcome to receive communion at a table thus "open". In the light of the ecumenical movement there are very many people who feel that this is just the kind of invitation that ought to be given, but nowadays, in view of the confusion that has arisen, it would be much more accurate if the invitation could be given *to all who are members of this Church or any other Church.*

Such a change would affect both the open and the closed communion Churches because it would have the effect in the open communion Churches of making the Table less "open", in that it would then be open only to baptized believers, and it would have the effect in the closed communion Churches of making the Table less "closed" in that it would then only be closed to those who were not baptized believers. This uniformity of understanding, without doing despite to the traditions of either side, would be a great step forward.

Another practical problem that arises when baptism is brought into close connection with membership is that of timing and the sequence of events. Here practice varies so much that it is impossible to state what is normal or most frequent. In some instances, a man may be baptized immediately on request to the minister provided he can satisfy the minister of his desire to be a disciple of Jesus Christ; he may or may not at this point have received communion and may or may not be seeking membership. In other cases, a man may only be baptized if his baptism is approved by the Church, in which case some delay is inevitable, though here too the Church may be unconcerned about anything other than his desire to be a disciple of Jesus Christ; again, reception of the communion and membership may or may not be regarded as important factors at this point. Sometimes, on the other hand, baptism may be taken seriously and a minister or Church will only baptize once they are satisfied that a candidate has had a good grounding in the faith. He may indeed have to appear before the Church, and it is more than likely that visitors will be appointed to interview him privately concerning his faith. This is more likely if membership is involved, in which case the candidate is usually received into membership of the Church at the first communion after his baptism, either by the laying on of hands or the right hand of fellowship. Such a service may be separated from the act of baptism either by hours or by

E

weeks, and if there are practical difficulties in arranging the baptismal service there are those who would receive the candidate into membership first and baptize him later.

Such wide variety of practice may shock many who are not themselves Baptists, and may even surprise some Baptists, but as there is tending to emerge a general pattern which does justice to the issues that really matter, it is in the interests of this common practice that certain matters must be stated.

If, for instance, baptism is the gateway to membership and is an important part of Christian initiation, then clearly the responsibility for baptism and membership must go together and be vested in the Church. Whether this should be the responsibility of the whole Church, vested in the church meeting, or whether it should be regarded as the responsibility of the whole Church, vested in the elders or deacons and/or the ministry of Word and sacrament, is another matter. This is an issue which has not yet been fully resolved theologically, and practice may therefore continue to vary. But what would appear fairly obvious on practical grounds is that the body responsible for the membership roll, for the admission of new members and for giving the authority for a baptism to take place, should be a regular continuing body. This gives uniformity of practice and consistency of approach, and ensures a body that is within the Church and in close touch with the membership. It would mean further that instead of an *ad hoc* appointment of visitors to candidates for church membership each Church would have certain people who were set aside for this important task. Such a step could profitably be taken at once in most Churches, though we may have to wait a while before we can see clearly whether the ultimate decisions should be taken by such a body or by the church meeting on the recommendation of such a body. Theologically, the two are quite different; in practice, they would usually be found to be the same.

Whoever makes the decision, the next point that arises is the conditions on which such a decision is to be made.

66

Put in its simplest form, a Church must be satisfied that a candidate for baptism has come to see, however vaguely, what God has done for him in Christ, and must have a desire to accept the relationship which God in Christ is anxious to confer on him, that of nothing less than eternal sonship. This in turn will involve accepting the Lordship of Christ and a readiness to become His disciple and to do His will, but this is much less important than the realization of what God is offering. Furthermore, it will be remembered that the candidate is presenting himself for initiation and not for perfection and therefore not too much must be required of him.

The grasping of this fundamental point then finds practical expression in the kind of training that is prescribed. When training takes place at all, it usually takes the form of a series of sessions of instruction by the minister. Such a course may occupy several weeks or even months and, although there is an increasing tendency today for it to continue after baptism, it is more usual for it to be completed before. During the training the candidate is likely to be given instruction on the nature of the Church, the history and principles of the denomination, the meaning of baptism and communion, with perhaps some simple guidance in the art of prayer, Bible study and worship, and although all these are issues of importance it is doubtful whether such a course covers the most important matters or deals with the issues at the most profitable time.

The aim of such training ought to be rather that of enabling the candidate to grasp and develop the basic conviction that he has when he applies for baptism. How can he grow more fully to appreciate what God has done for him in Christ? From this we have a direct line to worship: the candidate must be trained in the simple rules of worship and liturgy. He must see how in worship he offers himself to God and how in worship God forgives his sin and renews his life; he must see how this is not something which he alone does, but rather something he shares with his brethren in Christ. It is a corporate act. He must see further how liturgy is service as well as worship, and learn to understand what he is to offer to God on the other six days of the week. And through it all he must come to see these things not simply as intellectual things to be grasped with his mind but as matters that affect the whole of his life, body, mind and spirit. He must grow in the knowledge of God as he practises what he is taught, as a boy learns to play cricket not simply by receiving a course of instruction which he assimilates with his intellect, but rather by practising with a bat and a ball.

The analogy leads us to the thought of his teacher. In that part of the liturgy which relates to worship his most effective teacher may be his minister, for he is trained in the principles of liturgy as the cricket expert may be trained in the laws of cricket. But in that part of the liturgy that relates to service and life, what he really needs is a coach rather than a teacher, and here responsibility rests on those members of the congregation who have learned what it means to live the Christian life. The candidate must be trained to see his daily employment as his major act of Christian service and his chief offering to God, but he must also be brought to see how growth in the knowledge of God leads to growth in the care of His people.

Training for membership then comes to be seen not so much as a course of instruction at the end of which one could pass an examination, but rather as constant and steady guidance by one who has advanced on the Christian road for one who is just beginning. Ideally, training for membership continues until membership of the Church on earth is no more. But the time should come when the trainee is called upon to accept responsibility for the training of somebody else, though this will not mean that the days of his own training are at an end.

We have still not settled the issue as to how much training must be given before the baptism can take place and membership can begin. It is doubtful whether it can be settled. All that is needed is the willingness to co-operate on the part of the candidate and the willingness to care on the part of the membership. Spiritual growth is not something that can be produced; it is something that happens when the conditions are congenial.

Having thus dealt with the mechanics of admission to membership, we may now turn to the ceremony itself. Modern theology which links closely together baptism, church membership and communion, seeing the first as the gateway to the second and the second as the condition of the third, compels us to welcome the increasing tendency among Baptists to bring together baptism and communion in one service. Though thought by many to raise practical problems, it is not nearly such a big problem as is often imagined. The difficulties are usually alleged to arise at two points.

First is the matter of timing: a service of baptism and communion, it is maintained, is too long. Practicc has shown this difficulty unfounded. If readings and prayers are carefully planned, such a service need not last more than seventy-five minutes. A typical Order of Service for such an occasion is appended at the end of this chapter.

The second alleged difficulty is that of the time taken by the candidates to change. There are various ways of dealing with this and as yet there appears to be no clear understanding as to whether in such a service the baptisms should take place at the beginning or, in the more traditional place, after the sermon. The important point here is that the correct liturgical pattern should be preserved. Some clear statement of what is happening must precede the baptism, and if it is intended that this should be done in the sermon, then clearly the sermon must come first. On the other hand, this may be done in the form of a simple statement followed by a reading of scripture. In both cases, the candidate may see his baptism as a response to the word of God. If, then, the sermon follows the baptism it will tend rather to take the form of a charge to the newly-baptized. In either case, during the absence of the candidates the congregation may make its response to the word in the offering.[1] Suitable

---

[1] It might be more accurate to describe this as the collection, since the offering of the gifts and the elements must of course be kept for the beginning of communion.

hymns, the notices and possibly an anthem then help to bridge the gap and the candidates are ready to re-enter the Church.

The reception into membership at the beginning of communion is then seen not as a separate act but as the culmination of their baptism. The laying on of hands is at this point a biblical and an appropriate way of signifying the gift of the Holy Spirit in baptism and makes a very helpful distinction between those being received into membership for the first time and those who are being received in by the right hand of fellowship from membership of another congregation.

In the early days of the Church the bringing in of the bread and wine was the first act of the communion section of the service. The congregation stood to identify themselves with this offering and, together with the monetary gifts, it symbolized the complete offering of the congregation to God. Baptism was the act which qualified a man to present these offerings on behalf of the Church and it is therefore fitting that when the candidates return to the church after changing, they should bring with them the bread and the wine and, at the appropriate point in the service, present them to the presiding minister.

But what then in our present position are we to make of the unbaptized church member and the unbaptized communicant? To say that biblically and theologically there is no room for such people may be true, but it does not help at this particular juncture where we are essentially concerned with practical matters.

Perhaps the first thing is to reach a new understanding of what is meant by receiving members *on profession of faith*. In the past, this has tended to mean a declaration of faith before the gathered Church and has usually been regarded as an alternative to baptism. Sometimes the profession of faith is actually made, but at other times the very fact of presenting oneself before the Church for reception into membership is itself regarded as sufficient. Used occasionally for the sake of people who could not be immersed on medical grounds[1] it has tended too often to be an easier method for the nervous and the shy.

In the light of our present knowledge it would be more satisfactory if a specific order for profession of faith could be adopted and if it could be reserved for those who have been baptized in infancy but who had never come to faith or fulfilled the terms of membership for any branch of the Church. It is difficult to see how such a procedure could be objected to on the grounds that it seems to give partial recognition to infant baptism, since at present profession of faith alone is often regarded as adequate. It would, however, result in the abandonment of this practice and in the making necessary of some form of baptism, which would require us to insist on baptism where no form of it had ever been administered. This would of course be more difficult in practice than in theory, but if it were generally accepted as the direction in which we ought to move and if it were carefully applied in love by all the Churches, there is no reason why ultimately it should not become general practice.

Objections, however, would surely be raised even to the theory, and that from both wings. Closed membership Churches would object to it on the grounds that it was in fact membership without baptism; open membership Churches would object to it on the grounds that it required baptism. To the former it must be said that this is simply one of the anomalies which we must of necessity accept in the divided state of Christendom unless we still envisage the impossible concept that one day everybody is going to see things the way we see them. To the latter it must be said that if it is envisaged that baptism is to be the gateway to membership in any future united Church, this is one of the steps we can take now in order to draw nearer to our brethren.

Perhaps it would help our approach to this practical

---

[1] The adoption of more than one form of baptism is another way of meeting this problem, and might be much more satisfactory than dispensing with baptism altogether. There can be no theological significance in a medical certificate!

problem if we could bring ourselves to delineate the boundaries less clearly than we do at present. Generally speaking we point two categories of men, the saved and the unsaved, the converted and the unconverted, the Christian and the pagan; and then we identify these two classes with the church member and the non-church member. Such an approach arose very largely by way of reaction to the parish system which saw all the baptized within a given area as in membership with the local parish church. Neither conception really does justice to reality. Martin Thornton[1] says the parish system (as we have just defined it) fails to face the facts because it pretends that its parish is a uniform mass; the policy Baptists adopt, one of exclusion which extends beyond the nucleus only to a few faithful souls, faces the facts but evades the responsibility.

Thornton then shows how there are not two classes of people but three: first, the zealous minority; second, the enthusiastic supporters or the "up and coming"; third, the rest, whether spectators, apathetic or antagonistic. This pattern, he maintains, has constantly recurred through religious history. Judaism thought in terms of the world, the chosen race and the faithful remnant; the early Church centred in the Twelve, the proselytes and the world outside.

It is to this middle group that we need to give more urgent and practical attention. They need to be seen not as outsiders and pagans, nor yet as fully members and disciples of Christ. At present we have no alternative, and although we hesitate to refuse them full membership unless they are baptized, we find no difficulty in refusing them full membership until they have had a personal experience of Christ. A greater flexibility in the drawing of our boundaries, which saw these people as a part of the Church but as on the way to full discipleship, would help us to determine our initiation to membership more carefully, since it would not *ipso facto* appear to cut off all such people from the grace of God.

It is natural that when we first hear suggestions of this kind we should want to ask questions, and that any changes

[1] *Pastoral Theology: a Re-orientation*, 21.

that are made either in theory or in practice should be made with caution and hesitancy. It is, however, by asking questions and by groping forward in the darkness that we are able fully to discover the will of God, and it is only as each branch of the Church learns this for itself that we are likely to find ourselves growing nearer to each other, for the one thing which must be the same for us all is the will of God.

ORDER OF SERVICE
FOR A
BAPTISMAL EUCHARIST

The Baptism
    Statement on Baptism
    Baptismal Hymn
    Act of Baptism

The Preparation
    Hymn of Praise
    Prayers of Invocation, Confession and
        Assurance of Forgiveness

The Word
    Old Testament
    Psalm or Hymn
    New Testament
    Hymn
    Sermon

The Response
    Te Deum (reception of gifts)
    Prayers of Intercession

The Communion
    Offering of Alms and Elements
    Reception of Baptized into Membership
    Words of Invitation
    Sursum Corda

Prayer of Thanksgiving
Words of Institution
Fraction and Delivery
Lord's Prayer
Nunc Dimittis
Gloria in Excelsis
Hymn
Dismissal and Blessing.

The above order is compiled on the assumption that the baptisms will take place at the beginning of the service on analogy with the mission station where the baptisms often take place in the river followed by a service nearby.

In this order the candidates can usually return to the church during the hymn or psalm between the lessons, or during the hymn before the sermon.

For another order, based on the baptisms following the sermon, the reader is referred to Neville Clark, *Call to Worship*, 54 ff.

5

BAPTISM AND RE-BAPTISM

Such a sympathetic approach to infant baptism as we have just discussed comes up against further obstacles when it is suggested that those who have received baptism in infancy should not be permitted to receive baptism again as believers, not even if they desire it. It is one thing to give partial recognition to infant baptism to the extent of requiring some form of baptism as a condition of membership and of acknowledging that other form when it has already taken place. It is a vastly different matter to refuse believers' baptism to an individual simply because their parents chose to have them baptized in infancy.

Various objections to this procedure will be raised from a Baptist standpoint. For one thing, it cuts right across the Baptist understanding of the freedom of the individual soul before God; if a man, having come to God and seen from his reading of the scriptures the need to confess his faith in baptism, should request baptism, then it is alleged no minister or church has the right to refuse him. To brethren in other branches of the Church, where the arm of ecclesiastical authority wields a mightier power, and particularly where the individual is trained to accept the guidance of his spiritual director, this seems a strange and invalid attitude to the sacraments. So it may be. But it does nevertheless exist, and it is very difficult for those who have been reared on it, with generations of this approach behind them, to accept any other point of view without the feeling that they are denying their heritage.

Moreover, it is felt by many Baptists that to accept such a situation would in fact yield the death blow to believers' baptism. A large proportion (though perhaps not so large as used to be the case) of the children and young people who attach themselves to Baptist churches, but whose parents are not attached to any church, will in all probability have been baptized in infancy, and since in point of time one must always come before the other, the two forms of baptism can never therefore be regarded as straight alternatives. One, it is argued, must ultimately take precedence over the other, and because of the time factor there is said to be little doubt which one it will be. It is not often realized that the argument, if sound, is a tacit denial of all that is normally claimed for believers' baptism. Neither is it appreciated that at best it is an argument based on uncertainty. Those who believe that believers' baptism has a claim and a value all its own must realize that to deprive an individual of believers' baptism would of itself make that person think twice before baptizing his children, but such an attitude is justified only on a long term and requires much faith before one dare embark on it. It is a sad commentary on the attitude of many Baptists towards the subject that they are so clearly afraid to go forward in faith; their forefathers must have had considerably more faith to reject infant baptism in a day when no baptism meant no salvation.

Many Baptists again feel that such a step is not quite the same as giving a partial recognition to infant baptism; it is in fact acknowledging that infant baptism is baptism. To do this they feel is to deny their heritage. Baptism is the expression of one's faith by immersion. This infant baptism is not and cannot be. Therefore it is not baptism. To this we must return shortly. For the present suffice it to say that such an attitude does not merit serious discussion. One of the things we have learned in the last fifty years is to listen to one another; our biblical scholars and theologians have learned to come at these subjects afresh and to bridge the denominational fences that divide us in our parishes. To insist on building those fences so high that truth can never flow from one side to the other is to disown the good work which has been done. Baptism is clearly more than Baptists have traditionally understood by it. This does not mean that baptism is what the Anglicans or the Methodists have made of it and there is no question of giving up what we believe in order to do what they do. All that must be insisted on is that what they call baptism is baptism just as much as is what we understand by baptism. Both are defective, and progress is possible only if we are prepared to acknowledge that we each have a rite called baptism and a responsibility to go forward in an attempt to understand it together.

It is this recognition that requires us to refuse baptism to those who are baptized already on the grounds that baptism cannot take place twice. O. Cullmann,[1] for example, thinks that the point of John 13: 1–11 (the washing of the disciples' feet) is to counteract tendencies towards the repetition of baptism in the early Church, and other writers suggest that the baptismal context of Hebrews 6: 6 supports the interpretation of the Greek Fathers who asserted the impossibility of a second baptism. C. Spicq[2] draws the same conclusions from Hebrews 10: 26 f., and adds, "Just as Jesus cannot die anew, baptism cannot be repeated."

To all this there is no objection. Not even those Baptists who think that the freedom of the individual conscience is the be-all and end-all of the faith really believe in re-baptism. If a church member admits that he was baptized too young, or that he did not fully understand what he was doing, or that he has really had a conversion experience since, there are indeed few Baptists who would suggest that the rite should be repeated.

The bombshell bursts only when Neville Clark carries this idea to its logical conclusion with the words, "Finally, the re-baptism as believers of those who have received baptism in infancy constitutes a blow at the heart of the Christian faith."[3] For years Baptists have cheerfully baptized those who previously had been baptized in the Church of England or in one of the other Free Churches. To call a halt to such a practice would surely lead to an impoverishment of the Baptist understanding of the sacrament.

Though the problem itself is not a new one, the practical way in which it presents itself is quite modern. In the days when every denomination believed itself to be the only valid

[1] *Early Christian Worship*, 108.   [2] *L'Epître aux Hebreux*, ii, 321.
[3] A. Gilmore (ed.), *Christian Baptism*, 325–6.

expression of Christianity, when the members of one stead-
fastly refused to co-operate with the members of another,
when Churches of all denominations were found side by
side in every community however small, and when people
did not move from place to place so much as they do today,
the problem hardly arose. But now the ecumenical movement has drawn us all closer together and each acknowledges
the others to be part of the one Holy Catholic Church. Policies
of comity, practised for years on the mission field, have been
now accepted with regard to many new housing areas in
this country, and modern means of communication lead to
a constant shift of population.

The problem becomes real and practical therefore in four
ways. First, *on new housing estates*. It often happens that each
new housing estate has but one Free Church. Only occasionally, however, is such a church designated a Free Church;
it is more usual for it to retain its denominational affiliation,
on the understanding that it will not be exclusive. For
Baptists this has normally meant that the church must be
an open membership church so that Methodists, Congregationalists, and Presbyterians living on the estate may be free
to take up membership. Such people, it has been claimed,
could not be expected to fulfil the conditions laid down by a
closed membership trust.

In the light of what we said in the last chapter about open
membership and closed membership such a position is now
urgently in need of reconsideration. Such churches could,
and in our view ought really to, be open membership
churches only in the sense that they are open to all who
have been baptized and have come to faith in the Christian
Church, and not open to all believers regardless of baptism.
Up to now, many Baptists have recognized that we could
not expect such people to submit to baptism again. These
Baptists ought now to be bold enough to say that they ought
not and cannot. This is no academic issue; for many ministers
it is a very practical one. Either Baptists say, as they have
said, that baptism does not matter, or else they say that
baptism is essential though they are prepared to recognize

that in the present situation it need not be believers' baptism. This does not, however, preclude them in any sense from preaching believers' baptism nor need it prevent them from regarding believers' baptism as the norm.

Secondly, precisely the same situation exists *in older areas* where the only Free Church is a Baptist one, and since many of the older areas have undergone considerable re-development many of these places have in fact taken on the pattern of the new housing estate. Where these older Baptist churches had closed membership the position has become almost impossible; where they had open membership the inevitable tendency has been for believers' baptism to be threatened and sometimes even for baptism itself to become a secondary consideration.

In both these cases the problem may arise in such a way as to divide a family. A Baptist takes an Anglican wife and brings her home to his church; it is not easy to require that she be baptized in order to take up membership, but unless either some kind of honest recognition of her baptism is made or the whole rite of baptism is going to be devalued, then that is the only course. The same situation may be even more acute where a couple move into such a district and attempt to take up membership of such a church having come from membership in, say, a Congregational church, but where some years previously the wife had been baptized in a Baptist church and the husband had always been Congregationalist. Must Baptists insist on baptism for the husband, or do they say that baptism is unnecessary? Clearly they must do one or the other unless they can give some recognition to baptism as practised by the Congregationalists.

The third place where this problem arises is *in union churches*. Usually these churches are of joint Baptist and Congregationalist foundation, though sometimes in origin they include Methodists also. Provision was generally made for both forms of baptism and there would be the large baptistery for immersion and the font for christening. Links with the headquarters of both denominations would be preserved, both missionary societies would be supported and the ministry would be open to recognized ministers of either. It has often happened that Baptist and Congregationalist ministers have alternated and inevitably the emphasis tends to have swung to and fro according to the particular allegiance of either the minister or the leading officers. At some periods of the church's history believers' baptism has been preached and practised, at other periods the baptism of infants; and in some cases the result has been that no real attention has been given to baptism at all.

The main problem arises for the person who is born into one situation and grows up in another. A child, for instance, may be presented for baptism by parents who were formerly Congregationalists in a day when the minister was also Congregationalist. Seventeen years later, in the same church, but when now the ministry is Baptist, that youth has a conversion experience together with a number of other youths, some of whose parents were formerly Baptists and who therefore were not presented for baptism in infancy. Is the Baptist minister right to baptize them all in the same way? Should he encourage the one who has been baptized already to be baptized again? Or, even if such a person wants to be baptized like the others, should the minister endeavour to dissuade him on the grounds that it would be wrong to do so?

Fourthly, the problem becomes acute *in drawing up schemes of church union* like those of Ceylon, North India and Pakistan, Ghana, Australia and Wales. Here you are confronted with a union of Churches where previously both forms of baptism have been practised and where it is envisaged that provision for the continuance of both forms must be made in the constitution of the new united Church. Must it also be insisted that the door is left open for any who have been baptized as infants subsequently to be baptized as believers if they so desire?

Before we attempt to answer these questions, perhaps the problems ought to be sharpened in our minds. Basically, as we have seen, it is not really a question of re-baptism, for the teaching of the Christian Church throughout the centuries has been that baptism can only take place once and Baptists themselves have accepted the teaching. The issue is whether the sprinkling of an infant constitutes baptism. The early Baptists said that it did not, and some resented the nickname of Anabaptist[1] because they insisted that they were not *re*-baptizing; the people they baptized had not been baptized previously.

But if we are to say that infant baptism is "no baptism" then we are saying that for at least a thousand years the sacrament was not administered, and still is not administered in the greater part of Christendom. If true baptism is one of the essential marks of the true Church, then we are saying that for over a thousand years the true Church did not exist, and that the majority of people who today think they belong to it are under a serious misapprehension. In short, if infant baptism is "no baptism", then the Church that practises it is "no church". Few Baptists will want to go so far, and fewer still will find it possible to support such doctrines in practice.[2]

It is better to acknowledge that infant baptism, though partial in its expression of the truth and though involving serious theological distortion, is nevertheless baptism, and cannot therefore be followed by believers' baptism being administered to the same person.

In swallowing this somewhat bitter pill, however, there are one or two other points that ought to be noticed.

First, such an acknowledgment of infant baptism as partial and defective, though nevertheless baptism, is only basically the same kind of acknowledgment as the Baptist expects of the episcopalian with regard to his ministry. It is difficult to see how Baptists can be too indignant at the suggestion that their ministry is not a real ministry, requiring episcopal ordination before it can be, when in the next breath they are going to claim that infant baptism is not a real baptism, requiring believers' baptism before it can be. For either side

---

[1] Cf. E. A. Payne, *The Fellowship of Believers*, 72.
[2] This position was argued twenty years ago in R. C. Walton, *The Gathered Community*, 166.

to stick fast on both these points savours too much of "heads I win and tails you lose". If, in the interests of the unity of the Church, it is felt that the episcopalian should accept the Baptist ministry, even though he believes that it has not got all that the true ministry requires, then by the same argument the Baptist must be ready to accept infant baptism even though he believes it has not got all that true baptism requires.

To this it will no doubt be argued that this appears to be playing "tweedle-dum and tweedle-dee" with matters that are vital to the Church's life, and that such important issues cannot be settled by simply sliding over the difficulties. Such an argument presupposes, however, that the right answer has been found already and resides wholly on one side or the other. Such reasoning in our day is too naïve to be worthy of serious consideration and leads us to our second point.

The very inconclusiveness of the arguments for and against both forms of baptism ought to make us stop and think, and ought also to deliver us from a dogmatism that ill-becomes the scholar searching for the truth. No one who has read the literature on baptism during the last fifteen years could honestly feel that either side has really proved its point beyond a peradventure.

This inconclusiveness is further revealed if we turn from theology and argument to practice and experience. Here the analogy of the ministry helps us again to focus the issue. When the non-episcopal ministry of the Baptist churches is challenged by the episcopalians, the Baptist often replies that he cannot see how a Church could reject a form of ministry which God had so obviously accepted and signally blessed for over three hundred years, and which had been used by Him for the furtherance of the gospel all over the world. To the Baptist there appears to be considerable force in this argument from experience. What unfortunately many Baptists do not so readily appreciate is that precisely the same argument can be used of infant baptism. This has also been accepted by God and blessed by Him for well over a thousand years, and it would be a fool only who could maintain that infant baptism followed by faith has not been a means of grace to anyone.

Quite clearly, therefore, a partial acceptance of infant baptism as at present practised is not a selling of the whole gospel or even of that part of it for which Baptists have stood from the time of the Reformation, whilst a similar acknowledgment by Baptists of the partiality of their own rite as at present practised would be a sign of strength rather than weakness. To cease (in some such way as this) to regard the matter in terms of either/or and "blacks" and "whites" would be a great advance on the present situation. Is there not room in the providence of God for both forms of baptism to co-exist, and might not this inconclusiveness be one means by which God is seeking to lead His Church into something richer than our forefathers ever dreamed of?

This brings us to our third point. Believers' baptism was not the only principle on which the Baptists stood at the Reformation. They stood also for universal religious freedom and in their fight to achieve the truth as they saw it in the word of God they revealed (along with others) a spirit of courage and adventure such as the Church had scarcely known since the days of the apostles and martyrs. Thomas Helwys's *The Mystery of Iniquity* may be regarded as one of the first real pleas for religious toleration and their courage and adventure did not prevent them from turning their backs on things which their generation regarded as vital to salvation in order to establish what to them so clearly appeared to be the way forward.

It would be a pity if in their enthusiasm for the one principle of believers' baptism, important as it is, Baptists were to lose sight of the other two. The plea for toleration was a plea that people should be able to believe and worship according to their own understanding of scripture and knowledge of God.

If today Baptists are to recapture this spirit, it means that so long as those who practise infant baptism are convinced that this is the will of God for them, Baptists ought not to question their conviction of its validity. This point has been forcefully made by E. L. Wenger[1] in discussions on North India, but he also goes on to point out that it must not be thought that because Baptists tolerate infant baptism out of respect for those who regard it as valid, they in their hearts believe that it *is* valid. If my friend and I have joint possession of a motor car and he resolutely believes that in order to keep it in good running form it must be serviced every five hundred miles, the chances are that out of respect for this particular idiosyncrasy of his, I shall agree to his having it done. But my toleration of this fastidiousness does not in fact prove that he is right, neither does it suggest necessarily that I have been converted to his point of view. All it means is that if we are to hold something in common some kind of working arrangement must be made, and it would be a considerable help to all who are dealing with this problem at first hand if they could bring themselves to see this distinction and to live with it.

It will doubtless be pointed out here that such a situation is highly unsatisfactory and could not in fact be regarded as anything like a suitable solution to the problem. It is never intended that it should be. The early reformers did not see themselves as having arrived, but rather as being *en route*; it is to be regretted that what they regarded as a road has since come to be regarded as a destination. In the same way this state of mutual recognition and co-existence should not be seen as a final state to which one day we agree and in which we then live for evermore. It is rather a common platform from which together we can discern the will of God in the spirit of adventure which was so typical of the days of the Reformation.

Whilst it is impossible at this moment to see clearly the whole way that such common searching would lead us it is possible to see the occasional signpost. From the side of the Paedo-Baptists, for instance, much careful thought would need first to be given to the candidate for baptism. Whilst

[1] "The Problem of So-called Re-Baptism", in *Church Union: News and Views*, May 1958, 23.

there is much indiscriminate baptism, it is only to be expected that Baptists will insist that infant baptism, where practised, shall be treated more theologically and more seriously than it often is. From the side of Baptists, on the other hand, much careful thought would need to be given to those requirements that are sometimes made with regard to certain offices in the Church. Some Churches, for instance, make it a rule that a certain proportion of the diaconate must be baptized, and by that is usually meant baptized as believers by immersion; the same requirement is often, if not always, made of candidates for the ministry. Paedo-Baptists, therefore, at this point will naturally insist that such rulings be adjusted to the new situation so that re-baptism is no longer as it were written into the Baptist constitution.

But beyond such relatively obvious issues it is impossible to see where God might lead us in our thinking together. Neither is it necessary to see. We live by faith. If, now that we have come as near to each other as we have, this one particular move seems to us to be the will of God, then we must go forward, confident that God will reveal each successive stage to us as we are ready to receive it.

Finally, where both forms of baptism are to be practised in the one Church, and even where they are to co-exist by mutual arrangement in two parallel Churches, consideration will sooner or later have to be given to those cases where an individual has doubts about his baptism as an infant and asks for baptism as a believer. If this problem can be seriously tackled and a suitable arrangement made, the number of such cases may well be small; if it is not, or if the hand of law and order presses too hard, then the number is likely to increase and a further breakaway sect is by no means impossible.

The problem has been well focused and discussed in the *Plan of Church Union for North India and Pakistan* and we may as well deal with it in regard to this situation as deal in generalities. Appendix B to the Third Revised Edition (1957) purported to set out guiding principles with regard to the alternative practices of infant baptism and believers' baptism and held that since there is only one baptism, baptism is therefore unrepeatable in the life of any one person, no matter by which method it was administered. (This is the point which we have already stated should be the ideal.) It is further stated that ministers must not seek to persuade people who have been brought up on one form of baptism to adopt the alternative form for themselves or for their children, and guidance is given to ministers as to how those who profess a change of conviction with regard to baptism are to be dealt with. Here it is stated, in the event of a person already baptized in infancy being led to the conviction that believers' baptism is more truly in keeping with the mind of Christ, "the ministers of the Church will help such a person to seek the remedy of what he now believes to be a grave lack in his own Baptism, not by re-baptism, but by some other means which effectively re-affirms his Baptism and symbolizes for him his engrafting into Christ".

Thus far it is perfectly clear that re-baptism was to be excluded. The final clause of the Appendix, however, appeared to many to present a loophole. It read,

"It is further understood that, if a person should persistently maintain that only his Baptism now as a believer will satisfy his conscience, although he was baptized in infancy, the minister concerned will refer the matter to the Bishop of the Diocese for pastoral advice and direction."

It is around the meaning of the final phrase that discussion has ranged. To many Baptists it seemed to indicate a concession to the freedom of the individual conscience to the extent that a second baptism could take place if the case were approved by the bishop. To many Paedo-Baptists, however, the case seemed otherwise. Re-baptism had been so clearly ruled out in earlier clauses of the Appendix that it was impossible to imagine its re-appearing here. The final phrase permitted the bishop to do a number of things, none of which was specified, but the one thing it did not do was to permit him to agree to a second baptism. This restriction on personal freedom seemed so strong that it led many Baptists to doubt the wisdom of participating in such a united Church, fearing lest other similar and more serious restrictions might follow. As a result of prolonged discussion and negotiation it was proposed in early 1961 to deal with this problem by adding a note to the clause quoted above stating that this clause neither forbids nor implies any particular interpretation of the method of conscientious relief for a person baptized in infancy and afterwards desirous of believers' baptism. Since none of us knows the full truth on this matter this seems to us to be the only possible interpretation likely to commend itself.

When further discussions were held on the Continuation Committee in early 1964, it was apparent that some progress had been made. There were then those on all sides who were prepared to think of this as a pastoral problem with pastoral exceptions, and to recognize that though Appendix B states the rule of the Church it was not beyond the bounds of possibility that the Holy Spirit would lead otherwise. Perhaps the analogy of Christian marriage helps to point out the Christian responsibility. Here too the Church has a rule, and marriage is seen as a lifelong and indissoluble union; but here too the Church acknowledges pastoral responsibility when the rule has broken down. If union could be achieved on this basis, the Synod of the Church after union would have to work out the answer.

We have quoted this incident at length because it is the first attempt to come to grips with this situation and may well prove a model for others. Two points really need to be made.

First, in the situation in which we find ourselves some kind of concession must be made to the freedom of the individual conscience. To those who have been brought up in a more rigid church system, with pastoral guardians and directors, such a view seems both misguided and dangerous. Misguided it may be. It is, however, a fact that many people, and not only Baptists, believe in it and have been reared on it. Any failure to take account of it therefore is bound to lead to trouble. Dangerous also it may be, but it is doubtful whether it is as dangerous in practice as it appears to a stranger who is trying to understand it. It is true that it is an excessive amount of freedom that has presented the Baptist denomination with so many of its problems today, but this is an excess of freedom on the part of the local Church rather than on the part of the individual.

The two are not the same, and it is not suggested that freedom in this matter of baptism should rest with the local Church. The ultimate appeal, in the case of North India and Pakistan, was to the bishop. This in our view would be a quite proper procedure to adopt and it should be regarded as a very rare exception. Properly understood and carefully handled the problem may in the ultimate be more academic than real, but this will most certainly not be the case if the system is tied up too rigidly. Moreover, as has been insisted on already, the anomaly thus produced should never be regarded as anything more than a stage, even an unsatisfactory stage, in the process of growing together.

Secondly, and this from the Baptist side, some obvious attempt must be made to overcome the difficulty that arises when a person who has been baptized once, either as an infant or a believer, comes to have feelings of doubt about his baptism coupled with a desire to be baptized again. This situation already exists in Baptist churches, often in the case of a person who was baptized a little too young, or without fully understanding what it meant, or where a person has a religious experience after baptism and believes that baptism ought to be associated with it. Different ministers handle the situation in different ways, but it would certainly be rare for a Baptist minister to baptize someone a second time when his first baptism had been as a believer.

Because Baptists face this problem already they might begin to experiment even among themselves with some way of dealing with it. Experiences in South India have shown the need for such people, in penitence and faith, to affirm their belief, and that may possibly serve as a starting point. A form of service would have to be agreed upon and may profitably be used in the service of Holy Communion. Having thus said a definite "No" to Baptists who wished to be baptized again, an opportunity would nevertheless be provided for them to bear witness to their new faith before the congregation and also to express in public their repentance for their error. A similar form of service may also be used where a baptized believer has lapsed in his loyalties.

If it proved possible to develop and to practise such a rite then it may well help the situation in so far as those who were baptized as infants and who subsequently requested believers' baptism were concerned. No longer would it be a case of baptism or nothing, for a suitable alternative would be to hand. Furthermore, if it were felt, as it may well be, that some such rite faded into insignificance before believers' baptism, then it would only serve to enhance the ceremony which over the years has meant so much to Baptists.

So the ultimate issue becomes one of ecumenicity. The problems that are connected with re-baptism, and with practising both forms of baptism within the one Church, are not insuperable. Unless one is blissfully waiting for the day when everybody has become a Baptist, or when Baptists have ceased completely to count, some kind of attempt to deal with them must be made and be made at once. Moreover, it must be made in a spirit of Christian love and charity and in the light of the fulness of the gospel, remembering that the essence of the gospel is the grain of wheat that falls into the earth and appears to die before it can yield fruit. To erect barriers round any form of baptism, to the exclusion of all other forms, is in the ultimate to lose the one thing we are trying to safeguard. To be ready to lose it in the search for truth together with all Christian brethren is to be open to the one thing that God is seeking to give.

6

BAPTISM AND THE CHILD

THE relationship between the child and the Church is one which has never admitted of easy definition, though it has received increasing attention in recent years. The attacks of Brunner and Leenhardt, for example, have caused many Paedo-Baptist communities to think hard. The fruits of Methodist thinking have found expression in such works as those of H. G. Marsh[1] and W. F. Flemington,[2] whilst the fruits of Anglican thought have been revealed in a series of Reports[3] beginning in 1944 and continuing until the most recent one[4] which upholds adult baptism as the norm and infant baptism as the exception, and which declares that the incident of the blessing of infants (Mark 10: 13–16) has no obvious connection with baptism.[5]

But even to deny baptism to the child does not in fact solve the difficulty, as Baptists themselves have found out; indeed such a move serves only to sharpen the problem, for, if the child is not taken into the Body of Christ soon after birth, what then is his precise relationship with Christ and His Church?

Because Baptists have always put the emphasis on believers' baptism by immersion, they have had a better opportunity to consider this issue than those branches of the Church which have baptized infants and have therefore at any rate implied that such infants were part of the Body of Christ. What have Baptists made of such an opportunity?

The answer of the early Baptists appears to have been that no ceremony was needed for childhood at all, and, although there is some evidence for infant dedication or something

[1] *The Origin and Significance of New Testament Baptism* (1941).
[2] *The New Testament Doctrine of Baptism* (1948).
[3] *Confirmation Today* (1944), *Baptism Today* (1949), *Baptism and Confirmation Today* (1954), *The Theology of Christian Initiation* (1948), D. Gregory Dix, *The Theology of Confirmation in Relation to Baptism* (1946).
[4] *Baptism and Confirmation* (1958).   [5] Page xv.

similar in the eighteenth century, there does not appear to
be anything comparable to what we have today before the
beginning of the twentieth. This, when it was introduced,
arose mainly in response to popular appeal. R. L. Child[1]
traces its rise to John Clifford, who adopted it because so
many of his people desired to associate their children with
the Church and to seek its prayers just after their birth.
At first it was held in the home, but then (again in response
to a general desire) it was held publicly so that all members
could share in it.

It was not only the Baptists, however, who were governed
at this point by the *vox populi*. A. W. Argyle,[2] in his survey
of baptism in the early Christian centuries, says that one
factor in the transference of baptism from the believer to
the child was popular sentiment, expressed in a concern for
the welfare of children of Christian parents. Other branches
of the Church, moreover, who started without any such
ceremony, found they were continually under pressure of
this sort. The Churches of Christ, for instance, who also
rejected infant baptism in favour of believers' baptism, have
also for several generations now used a simple form of public
thanksgiving and prayer for parents and their infants. So,
too, did "The Barton Preachers", a group of evangelical
Christians in Leicestershire who adopted the sentiments of
the Baptists in 1755, and the Paulicians of the ninth century,
a group in the Eastern Church who denied the validity of
infant baptism but who nevertheless had a ceremony for
the blessing of infants. It was held on the eighth day after
birth in the home of the child and in the presence of the
members of the congregation; they said together the Lord's
Prayer and then offered a prayer for the blessing of the child
and prayed that he might be "brought through" to reach
baptism.

Whilst on strictly biblical and theological grounds therefore, it may be asserted that no ceremony for infants is
required, experience shows that, where there is no ceremony

[1] *The Blessing of Infants and the Dedication of Parents*, 3–5.
[2] A. Gilmore (ed.), *Christian Baptism*, 189.

to be found, it is necessary to invent one. This was forcefully put by Neville Clark,[1] when he wrote,

> "From the earliest times infant baptism has been a practice in search of a theology . . . we may reject the theory . . . but we may not therefore assume that the instinct of the church was necessarily at fault. History has repeated itself. Among the Baptists in recent decades there has grown up the practice of the blessing of infants. Again it arose in response to popular Christian demand. Again, it has been, more or less unsuccessfully, in search of a theology ever since."

It is indeed only recently that Baptists have made any serious attempt to understand and to interpret this legacy of infant dedication and even then they have shown little imagination and little desire to break new ground. The first person to embody the rite in a set form was M. E. Aubrey,[2] who took as his basis the bringing of the children to Jesus by their mothers, and who then went on to interpret it as a consecration of parenthood. Thanksgiving is there, but is always overshadowed by the importance of the parents' responsibility. Blessing takes place, but is quickly followed by a brief intercessory prayer on behalf of the child. The Church has no part other than that of welcoming the child and sharing with the parents in thanksgiving and supplication. It was in its day an attempt, one ought to say a most valiant attempt, to restore order out of chaos. Its value may be judged by the fact that it has never really been superseded and that this is the interpretation of infant dedication now most widely held by Baptists. M. E. Aubrey can scarcely be criticized because he did not produce a rite which gave due emphasis to the points considered to be important in the middle 60's.

If from these early days, however, the meaning of infant dedication has been increasingly consistent, the practice over the years has been chaotic. In some churches the rite has

[1] A Gilmore (ed.), *Christian Baptism*, 320-1.
[2] *A Minister's Manual.*

never been used at all and in some it has only begun to win its way in the post-war era. In others it has been widely used and has been open to all who chose to come, despite the fact that the promises made by the parents in the service are solemn promises. In other places again it has been reserved for the children of church members or those very closely linked with the church's life.

The place and circumstances have been no less varied. As far as one can tell, the service has normally taken place at the close of the Sunday morning service in the presence of the congregation, but such practice has been by no means universal. Often it has taken place in the Sunday school and sometimes in the home. In some instances it has even been known for children of church members to be dedicated in church, and children whose parents never came to worship to be dedicated in the Sunday school, much the same service being used in both instances. Some ministers have never dedicated more than one baby on each occasion; others have waited until several could be dedicated together. Some have taken the baby from the mother for the blessing and then given him back to the father; others have simply laid their right hand on the baby's forehead; others again have done both, and some neither.

Whilst in such a ceremony there is room for some variety of practice, it is hard to resist the conclusion that in this instance variety has rather got the bit between its teeth. Add to this the slender foundation on which the rite was originally introduced, together with the loose connection between the foundations of the rite and the rite as it developed, and it is abundantly clear that the time for some new thought has arrived.

With the passing of time the main element of M. E. Aubrey's service (i.e. dedication of parents) has undoubtedly stolen the stage, with the element of thanksgiving acting as a kind of "under-study". In some quarters there has been an attempt to get rid of all references to infant dedication and to think rather of thanksgiving for the birth of the child and the dedication of the parents. R. L. Child called his pamphlet on the subject, *The Blessing of Infants and the Dedication of Parents*, but the reference to "blessing" was thought injudicious by some and hence the stress on thanksgiving persisted.

Coupled with this emphasis on the parents' dedication, however, there has also gone a desire to make the ceremony more worthy of the occasion and therefore to pay more attention to it. A new appreciation of blessing and thanksgiving has also arisen, partly as a result of biblical theology, and so the three elements have come to appear side by side with a greater balance of emphasis. This in turn has brought its own problems.

The ideal service of the older order, giving due emphasis to all three sections, has now been given to us by J. O. Barrett, who adds to it a little commentary, which can be of value to parents.[1] The weakness of the foundations, however, now becomes quite apparent in a way that it did not when the burden of the services related to the parents. As long as the service gave the chief attention to the parents and their promises, thanksgiving and blessing taking a subsidiary role, this was essentially a service for the children of Christian parents. It might at times be pertinent to ask whether it was in fact necessary to bring the child along for something that appeared to concern him so little, but since it was out of a desire to bring the child that the service had arisen this query was not raised and the lack of coherence was rarely noticed. It might also be pertinent at times to refuse dedication to the child of parents who quite clearly had no intention of fulfilling the vows they were taking, but this was such a delicate business that it was usually deemed better to accept the dedication in the hope of winning the parents. But both these were minor difficulties. At least it was clear what the service was for.

The real difficulty arises when, as in Barrett's order, you elevate the thanksgiving and the blessing to a position of equal importance, for these surely are (or ought to be) for all children. The one half demands the Christian home,

[1] *Your Child and the Church.*

profession, discipleship; the other half seems to indicate, if not justify, indiscriminate reception.[1] Here is a sign of our theological confusion and a very real problem as a result.

An attempt to rectify this has been made by S. F. Winward[2] and finds expression in the new service book edited by him and E. A. Payne.[3] Winward is clearly not afraid of the idea of dedicating infants and maintains that if you give thanks over a child then that child is dedicated or holy to the Lord. The second part of the service consists of the promises, of which there are two, one made by the parents that they will give the child a Christian training, and one made by the Church, accepting some responsibility for their share in the child's Christian training. Finally comes the blessing, based on the blessing of infants by Jesus, to which is attached great significance. It is followed by a prayer that the spirit of God may work in the child, so looking forward to conversion.

Such an approach is bolder and rests on firmer biblical foundations than previous orders that have been suggested. It attaches a quite new significance to the rite in that the child who has been so dedicated clearly stands in a different relationship to God from one who has not; not in the sense that he is privileged, but in the sense that Israel was different; that is, different because he is chosen of God and given a responsibility.

Nevertheless it still fails to come to grips with the main problem. For whom is this service intended? The thanksgiving can surely be engaged in by everyone to whom a child is born; and in a sense, once the thanksgiving has taken place, the parents are obliged to answer yes to the promises, for to make a child holy to the Lord is to acknowledge a responsibility to ensure that he grows up to know God. Yet can all this be attributed to and legitimately expected from all the parents who bring their children to us

[1] This point is brought out in a review by Neville Clark in *Baptist Quarterly*, xviii (1959–60), 335–6.
[2] *The Dedication of Your Child.*
[3] *Orders and Prayers for Church Worship.*

for dedication? And if not, on what basis do we agree or not to the performance of the rite?

Understood in this sense, Winward's order is an advance in that it does at least limit dedication by relating the whole service to the same group of people, though whether he has in fact limited it to the right group is another matter to which we must return presently. The order fails, however, mainly because of its lack of objectivity. It is too much concerned with us and our children and what we do for them, and too little concerned with a child as a child of God and what God has done for him.

This matter has been tackled by Neville Clark[1] who has tried to build up his approach beginning with a new theology of childhood. He makes three points. First, we must distinguish between believers (and their children) and unbelievers (and their children), the former belonging to the sphere of the Body of Christ, the latter belonging to the world which is marked by the seal of redemption. Secondly, we must distinguish further between believers and their children. To the believers the word of God has been addressed and a response has been solicited. Their children, by birth, are specially related to the Body of Christ, but the relationship is not to be understood in terms of God's dealing with lost humanity. It stems rather from the fact of Christian marriage and is manifested in the influences of grace which constantly press upon such infants as they grow amid the ceaseless commerce of Church with home and home with Church. Therefore, and thirdly, baptism is not at all relevant at this stage.

What is relevant, however, is a ceremony based on the blessing of the infants by Jesus in the gospel story, but concerned not with human vows, human acts, human promises, so much as with the recognition and declaration of an act of God, by which a child has been specially related to the redeemed community, and with the claim and demand which that *opus dei* imposes upon Church and parents alike. "All this the rite should express."

Such a solution seems to us to have a more consistent

[1] A. Gilmore (ed.), *Christian Baptism*, 321 ff.

approach than any other and has the great advantage that it is quite clear for whom such a service is intended even if pastorally it presents a number of difficulties. Nevertheless, one cannot help but still wonder whether in fact any ceremony is needed at all to mark this special relationship which the children of Christian parents have with the Body of Christ. Certainly such an interpretation cannot spring out of the blessing of infants by Jesus, any more than can the order and interpretation with which we are now familiar. And unless "Christian parents" is to be interpreted in its widest sense, then such a ceremony would appear to limit the use of the rite in a way that it has not been limited elsewhere. Ceremonies connected with birth or with infancy are normally open to all of the tribe or religion concerned, since they deal with the fundamental fact of birth rather than with a particular interpretation of it. Clark's thesis, unless *we* narrow it unduly, seems to relate to Christian marriage rather than to birth.

But if the Baptists are confused and at variance in such matters, so also are the other branches of the Church. This, far from being a consolation, does in fact only add to the confusion. The minister or Church which has read nothing and which has stuck rigidly to one order is at least content; for the minister and Church that are alive to the issues the problems often seem insoluble.

In view of this, and in view of the fact that infant dedication has never been at the heart of Baptist teaching, there is something to be said for discontinuing the practice until some kind of ecumenical thinking can take place and some kind of common policy can be worked out with other denominations, but because this policy is not likely to commend itself to anyone, we succumb to the temptation of taking further the line suggested by Clark. What sort of order would it give us?

Attention would need to be paid to four points. First, there must be an act of thanksgiving for a child born to Christian parents, and therefore born into this special relationship with the Body of Christ through the fact of

Christian marriage. Secondly, there must be a declaration of what God has already done for the child before the child could do anything for God; this, however, must go further than a declaration of the child's place in the love of God, a fact that is shared with every other child, and must declare the particular relationship which this child is to have with the Church because of the fact that he is born to Christian parents. Thirdly, there must be a prayer of invocation that God will enable the child to realize to the full the special benefits and blessings with which he has been endowed. Fourthly, there must be a response on the part of the parents and the Church, not exactly as to what they will do for the child, but as to how they will themselves continue to wait upon God so that he may bring to full fruition the work he has already so obviously started.

In such a service there would be nothing that is out of harmony with Baptist principles, though the approach would be quite different from what Baptists already have. In this instance, however, the problem of a change of emphasis should not be so great as in the case of baptism, the Lord's Supper and independency.

Furthermore there are some indications that certain Anglicans would like to see changes similar to those here propounded. For them the difficulty of experiment is obviously greater because in their case it is the rite of baptism that is at stake. Yet even so the difficulties may not be so formidable as is sometimes imagined. E. C. Whitaker[1] quotes Bishop Frere's principle of liturgical revision that "the man in the pew is a conservative", and acknowledges that on these grounds it is the duty of those who create new rites to consider the people who have grown old in the Church's worship and who do not easily adapt themselves to new ways. But he then goes on to maintain that this principle is scarcely relevant to the matter of baptism since the average lay person probably does not attend more than half a dozen baptisms in his lifetime, and if a new service were introduced he would scarcely notice the difference. There is,

[1] *The Proposed Services of Baptism and Confirmation Reconsidered*, 9.

however, an increasing tendency towards public baptism and if this is to continue the years for revision may be few.

This, together with the recent Report,[1] discussed previously, are all encouraging signs, but the fact still remains that it is easier for the Baptists than for anyone else to experiment at this point, though if Baptists could satisfactorily break new ground there is reason to believe that others would be glad to take advantage of it.

The more important issue is that of determining whether in fact Clark's emphases are the right ones. Whilst we believe that his contribution delivers us from the wrong lines and points us in the right direction, we are of the opinion that it needs to be linked with some fresh thinking on the status of children that has been going on in other quarters in order to arrive at a more satisfactory conclusion.

G. W. Rusling,[2] for instance, has argued that the child should be seen as a catechumen in the sense that he is under instruction, is participating regularly in Christian worship and is on the way towards church membership. In some cases such children will be there under the guidance of their own parents and in other cases they will be under the guidance of a Sunday school teacher, a junior church leader or some other church member standing *in loco parentis*. In this respect there is no difference between the child of a pagan home and the child of Christian parents; the domestic setting may be different, but in regard to the Church and its ancillaries they stand side by side. Both share the love of God and both have been born into a world for which Christ died. He then pleads for an infancy rite which could include everything that can be legitimately said and done for children in infancy, and argues that if our dedication service does not do this already it is at least capable of doing it.

This would call for a widespread practice of infant dedication to all and sundry which would be quite contrary to current trends in the Church as a whole and the opposite of

---

[1] *Baptism and Confirmation.*

[2] "The Status of Children", in *Baptist Quarterly*, xviii (1959–60), 245–57.

what Baptists have done previously, but, as Rusling himself points out, it is difficult to square the insistence on infant baptism as a demonstration of prevenient grace and the desire to restrict it to children of Christian parents.

On the basis of 1 Corinthians 7: 14 he next proceeds to show that these children by their links with Christian parents or with Christians who stand *in loco parentis* are to be regarded as holy to the Lord; holiness in this context not to be regarded as moral quality but rather as an objective relationship with God. The fact that the child's "holiness" does not derive from physical contact with his parents is defended on the grounds that it must also apply to children taken for adoption and this in turn supports his thesis that it can apply to those who stand *in loco parentis* in the Church.

This is slightly wider than Clark's contention that the relationship of the child with God stems from the fact of Christian marriage, but still adheres to his main point that there must be a distinction between those children who have been presented to God in this way and those who have not. What Clark asserts only of the children of a Christian marriage Rusling asserts of all children who stand in a close relationship with a Christian family.

The bringing together of these two points of view now gives us a clue as to the way forward. In infant dedication we are to be concerned primarily with the child and his relationship to God and not with parents and their parental responsibilities. Further we are concerned with what God has done for the child and not with what the child one day will do for God. But God's work for the child is not simply something that is past. It is also present and future. To speak of the child's relationship with God, therefore, is not simply to assert what God *has* done, but what God *is* doing in the act of presentation and what God *will* do through his faithful disciples in the Church.

Once this is grasped it at once becomes desirable that children in general and not simply children from practising Christian homes should be brought for dedication. This, at any rate, is no more open than the occasion when Jesus received the children who were brought to Him and on which everything else is normally built. In the ceremony, care must be taken to state clearly the concern and love of God for all human life and the desire that all life should belong to Him.

What is then asserted must be realized. The child, who has been given to God and who has been blessed by the prayers of thanksgiving of the Christian Church, must be set within the Christian family as a catechumen. If his parents (or one of his parents) are themselves members of the Church this is comparatively easy since the influences of the home will be one with the influences of the Church, the worship of the one will find fuller expression and continuation in the worship of the other, and positive Christian training will take place in both places side by side.

In the case of children whose parents are not actually members of the Church the situation is less straightforward. If the new relationship with God, conferred in dedication, is to mean anything it must find practical expression in a relationship with the Christian Church. Some family in the Church must "adopt" the child. In so "adopting" the child this family will be accepting a certain responsibility for his Christian training, attendance at worship, and so on, but this is incidental to their true function. They are "adopting" the child primarily in order that his new relationship with God, declared in dedication, may become realized in a relationship with God's people. So that just as one becomes a Christian, not by baptism nor by faith, but by baptism and faith together resulting in full membership within the people of God, so one becomes a catechumen, not by something which God has done apart from us nor by a ceremony of dedication, but by a ceremony of dedication resulting in an actualization here on earth of what God has done in eternity: namely, a relationship with Him through His people.

This "adopting" of children by Christian families is not to be confused with the idea of god-parents, nor dismissed with it either. The Church is not undertaking to give the child a Christian education, neither is it promising to see to it that the child grows up to know, to love and to serve

God. None of these things, as we know full well, can in fact be honestly promised since there is no certainty that the promises can be fulfilled. The Church is declaring and acknowledging a relationship. If the relationship is maintained it is impossible to believe that ultimately the love of God will not make its own claim upon the child's life.

This does not mean, however, that the training of such catechumens should be left entirely to chance. It is true that our own children learn more by what they see of us than by what we consciously teach them, but this does not exclude positive teaching. And no more need it exclude positive teaching in the church, though it would be a mistake to attach too much importance to it. The child's period as a catechumen is a prolonged one and his training comes more from his parents than from the minister or church officers.

There would therefore appear to be good reason for transferring much of the effort that goes into teaching children and training teachers and leaders into similar attempts to guide and train parents in bringing up children in the Christian way of life. So far this is rather unploughed territory. Many even of the best parents find it difficult to discuss with their children the main principles of Christian worship, the significance of baptism and the Lord's Supper and the essentials of faith, love and prayer. If, too, the child receives teaching different from that of a previous generation, discussion at home becomes well-nigh impossible. To this may also be added the difficulty of teaching children simply to pray. Not only is there a shortage of books on the subject but some of those that exist are positively bad, and many parents would find it hard to sift the wheat from the chaff. Moreover, there is still much thinking to be done on the place of worship in the home and the most effective ways of teaching children simple moral and religious truths.

If the whole of childhood is a prolonged period of training, it is parents primarily who need guidance in these matters, and this is a case where to appear to neglect the training of the child for the sake of helping the parents will in the long run prove to be to the benefit of all. Experience also suggests that where parents of young children are offered this kind of guidance and instruction they are more than ready to avail themselves of it.

Where children who have been dedicated have parents who do not attend church, and where their attachment therefore is to some other member of the church, the matter is even more difficult, whilst being at the same time more vital. The Church has yet to think out ways in which such members can influence, help and guide the lives of those children who belong to them in Christ. Part of the principle of Family Church policy is that every child whose parents do not attend church should have some such attachment, though in practice it is often one part of the Family Church which fails to work. It is an open question whether such attachments without Family Church would not be more beneficial than Family Church without such attachments, though few would deny that the ideal is both.

If a Church could satisfactorily follow out such a plan of campaign, dedicating children quite freely, attaching them realistically to the Church and training them systematically all through their childhood up to the point of membership, it would soon become irrelevant to ask whether dedication made any difference and whether children who were dedicated were in any sense different from children who were not. The facts would be apparent for all to see, but the differences would still essentially be those of responsibility rather than privilege, and as the years passed by the child would be able to grow naturally into his responsibilities as he took his rightful place in the Church.

In order to clarify what we have been saying about infant dedication we give below an outline Order of Service, in skeleton form, embodying the main issues.

ORDER OF SERVICE FOR
INFANT DEDICATION

(*To follow the opening hymn and prayer at morning worship*)

Let us hear the words of scripture which are our warrant for holding this service:

Hear, O Israel; the Lord our God . . . and when you rise.

(Deuteronomy 6: 4–7. R.S.V.)

And they were bringing children to him . . . Laying his hands upon them.

(Mark 10: 13–16. R.S.V.)

Here in the word of God we are confronted with the concern and love of God for all human life and with the desire that all life shall belong to Him. In the action of Jesus we see the readiness with which He regards all children as belonging to the kingdom of God.

Therefore following the will of God and the example of our Lord we are pleased this morning to receive ───── in company with *his* parents. We welcome them as Jesus welcomed the children and their mothers in the days of His flesh. We join the parents in thanksgiving for the new life which God has granted to them, and we bless Him for a child born and brought into His house and dedicated to Him with thanksgiving.

We remember what God has done for this His child in Jesus Christ. We acknowledge His love and care for *him* at this moment. And in faith we know that through the fellowship of His Church He is able to lead *him* to the fulness of faith.

Therefore in receiving this child in this way we acknowledge *his* relationship with God expressed in fellowship with His Church and pledge ourselves to maintain this relationship until this child becomes His by faith and baptism:

At this point the minister shall receive the child into his arms to signify the child's reception into the family of God. The congregation

*shall stand in token of welcome. After saying the child's full name
the minister shall repeat the blessing:*

The Lord bless thee and keep thee; the Lord make His
face to shine upon thee, and be gracious unto thee; the Lord
lift up His countenance upon thee, and give thee peace. *Amen.*

*The minister shall return the child to his father, and there follow
prayers of intercession for the child, the Church and the home. There
may also be a suitable hymn.*

INDEX

A. SUBJECTS

B. AUTHORS